Meta-Analysis of Finance and Growth in Asia

Amar Anwar · Ichiro Iwasaki

Meta-Analysis of Finance and Growth in Asia

Making Sense of Globalization

palgrave
macmillan

Amar Anwar
Shannon School of Business
Cape Breton University
Sydney, NS, Canada

International SEPT
Competence Center
Universität Leipzig
Leipzig, Germany

Ichiro Iwasaki
Department of Law, Economics
and Management
Okinawa University
Naha, Okinawa, Japan

Institute of Economic Research
Hitotsubashi University
Tokyo, Japan

ISBN 978-3-032-10218-8 ISBN 978-3-032-10219-5 (eBook)
https://doi.org/10.1007/978-3-032-10219-5

This Palgrave Macmillan imprint is published by the registered company Springer Nature Switzerland AG.
The registered company address is: Gewerbestrasse 11, 6330 Cham, Switzerland

To my beloved wife, Arshia Khalid, and my daughter, Zoha Amar

—Amar Anwar

To my wife, Naoko

—Ichiro Iwasaki

Acknowledgments This book would not have been possible without the generous support of several institutions and funding bodies. Amar Anwar gratefully acknowledges financial support from the Cape Breton University RISE Grant (RISE 81306), which provided essential resources for research, analysis, and manuscript preparation. Ichiro Iwasaki acknowledges financial support from the Japan Society for the Promotion of Science (JSPS KAKENHI Grant Number: 25K04997), which supported the analytical and methodological components of this work. We are also grateful to our affiliated institutions—Cape Breton University, Universität Leipzig, Okinawa University, and Hitotsubashi University—for fostering a collaborative academic environment and supporting cross-national research initiatives. Finally, we extend our heartfelt thanks to our families and colleagues for their encouragement, patience, and thoughtful feedback throughout the writing of this book.

Summary of the Project

This book offers a systematic and empirically grounded reassessment of the relationship between financial development, globalization, and economic growth in Asia. While the finance–growth nexus has long been a staple of development economics, empirical findings remain inconclusive, and the influence of globalization is still poorly understood. Asia—with its diverse institutional landscapes, varying levels of financial maturity, and contrasting reform trajectories—provides a unique context to explore these complexities.

This study synthesizes the finance-growth literature across South and East Asia, drawing on a meta-analysis of 79 empirical studies and 759 effect-size estimates. It goes beyond traditional synthesis by accounting for methodological heterogeneity, examining structural moderators (e.g., institutional quality, financial liberalization), and testing for publication selection bias. The use of advanced meta-regression tools—such as Bayesian Model Averaging (BMA), Weighted-Average Least Squares (WALS), and bias-correction estimators—ensures robustness and transparency.

Key findings reveal that financial development is positively associated with growth in Asia, but the effects vary substantially by context. South Asia demonstrates stronger marginal gains, particularly in settings where financial access is widening and institutional capacity is improving. By contrast, East Asia—despite its financial sophistication—shows signs of saturation and increased volatility, especially in cases where liberalization preceded the development of robust regulatory frameworks. Crucially, globalization—measured through proxies such as capital account openness and stock market liberalization—does not uniformly enhance growth. Rather, it operates as a conditional moderator, either strengthening or weakening the impact of finance depending on institutional quality and the sequencing of reforms.

The book challenges the "one-size-fits-all" model of financial reform. Rather than promoting generic liberalization, it argues for a context-sensitive approach grounded in institutional capability, policy sequencing, and developmental needs. Policymakers are urged to prioritize financial inclusion, macroprudential oversight, and digital transformation as strategic levers for inclusive growth.

Methodologically, the book demonstrates the value of meta-analysis as a tool with direct implications for policy design and evaluation. By distilling insights from a wide array of studies, it highlights not only what the literature gets right, but also where it falls short—particularly in addressing inequality, financial fragility, and the unintended consequences of globalization.

This study offers several policy-relevant insights for financial sector reform across Asia's diverse economies. First, it underscores the importance of sequencing liberalization behind regulatory readiness, particularly in contexts where premature openness can amplify volatility and destabilize financial systems. Second, it highlights the growth potential of digital financial inclusion, especially in underbanked regions of South Asia, where even modest improvements in access can deliver substantial returns. These findings reinforce the case for policy frameworks that are not only market-deepening but also institutionally grounded and context-sensitive. Third, the findings suggest that institutional quality is a precondition—not a byproduct—of effective financial development; without credible governance, finance may reinforce inequality or fragility. Finally, the evidence cautions against one-size-fits-all reform templates, advocating instead for context-sensitive strategies that align financial structure with technological capacity, macroeconomic goals, and development stage.

In sum, this book offers a timely and rigorous contribution to debates on finance and development in Asia. It provides researchers, policymakers, and development practitioners with a framework to navigate the complexities of financial reform in a region marked by institutional diversity, economic ambition, and growing global integration.

Contents

List of Figures

List of Tables

CHAPTER 1

Introduction—Why Finance and Growth in Asia Still Matter

1.1 Rationale and Motivation

Asia's economic ascent over the past five decades is among the most significant transformations in modern development history. From Japan's early industrial ascent and the rise of the Four Asian Tigers to China's scale-driven industrialization and India's services-led surge, the region's experience has challenged conventional development theories. Across these varied trajectories, one constant has been the role of finance. Financial systems—whether bank-based, market-led, state-directed, or digitally driven—have both enabled and mirrored broader economic transitions.

Yet the relationship between finance and growth in Asia remains contested. Classical economists such as Schumpeter (1911) emphasized a "supply-leading" role, where finance fosters innovation and reallocates resources efficiently. In contrast, the "demand-following" perspective, rooted in Robinson (1952), posits that finance merely adapts to real-sector growth. Empirical evidence from Asia has not decisively confirmed either position. Instead, the finance–growth nexus appears complex, context-specific, and shaped by institutional and structural differences.

In some Asian economies, financial development has preceded and catalyzed growth. Singapore's rise as a financial hub, Korea's targeted credit allocation to strategic industries, and Malaysia's capital market reforms are cases where finance was deliberately used as a tool of transformation.

A. Anwar, I. Iwasaki, *Meta-Analysis of Finance and Growth in Asia*,
https://doi.org/10.1007/978-3-032-10219-5_1

In contrast, India's financial system has evolved alongside its services-led growth rather than driving it. In others, such as Pakistan or Myanmar, periods of financial expansion have not consistently translated into inclusive growth or productivity gains.

State intervention adds another layer of complexity. China exemplifies a state-directed financial model where tightly regulated banks and credit controls have fueled capital formation. While this model enabled rapid growth, concerns over misallocation, financial repression, and systemic risk have emerged. Ye et al. (2023) stress the importance of aligning financial structures with evolving technological needs, warning that structural mismatches can constrain even high-saving economies. These concerns are particularly relevant in Asia, where diverse financial systems coexist with rapidly shifting modes of production and value creation.

Historical experiences highlight the dual nature of finance as both opportunity and risk. The 1997 Asian Financial Crisis revealed the dangers of premature liberalization, weak regulation, and capital flow volatility. In response, many Asian economies undertook reforms, including the development of local currency bond markets and strengthened financial supervision. Still, the challenge persists: how to harness the benefits of financial openness while avoiding its risks. Haini et al. (2023), using cross-country data, find that financial integration supports growth only up to a threshold, beyond which openness can dampen the positive effects of finance and institutions. These findings underscore the risks of crowding out domestic intermediation and heightening macro-financial vulnerabilities.

The nature of financial development is also changing. Asia has emerged as a global leader in financial innovation, from India's Unified Payments Interface (UPI) to the rapid expansion of fintech in China and mobile banking in Southeast Asia. These shifts are enhancing financial inclusion and efficiency, often bypassing traditional banking systems. At the same time, they introduce new regulatory concerns. Isayev and Farooq (2024) document the rise of shadow banking and its implications for financial stability. While these innovations expand credit access, they often escape regulatory scrutiny, adding complexity to the finance–growth relationship in the region.

Given Asia's institutional and structural diversity, interpreting the finance–growth nexus through a single lens is inadequate. Asteriou et al. (2024) show that in Europe, this relationship is both time-variant and institution-sensitive, influenced by fiscal conditions and stress episodes. Similarly, Wang et al. (2023) demonstrate that the effect of financial openness depends on a country's income level and institutional maturity. These studies resonate with the Asian context, where governance quality, macroeconomic management, and development stage all shape financial outcomes.

Asia's heterogeneity—ranging from high-income financial hubs like Singapore and Hong Kong to financially underdeveloped lower-middle-income countries—presents both an opportunity and a challenge for research. The region encompasses both liberalized and capital-controlled markets, stock market–oriented systems, and state-dominated banking sectors, and countries with extensive financial services alongside others where access remains limited. This diversity offers a fertile ground for empirical inquiry but also demands analytical tools capable of synthesizing variation across methods, models, and contexts.

This study addresses that need by systematically synthesizing the empirical literature on finance and growth in Asia. Drawing on a meta-analysis of 79 empirical studies and 759 effect-size estimates, it seeks to bring coherence to a fragmented body of research. Rather than advancing a single conclusion, the study maps empirical regularities, identifies key moderating factors, and highlights areas of divergence.

We incorporate methodological heterogeneity into our meta-analytic framework. Recognizing that reported effects vary depending on estimation choices—such as functional form, dynamics, and estimation strategy—we differentiate between linear and nonlinear models and assess how methodological decisions influence effect-size estimates. We also examine the role of globalization, institutional quality, and regional variation as moderators to better understand the conditions under which finance fosters or fails to foster growth.

The study is timely and policy-relevant. As Asian economies confront post-pandemic recovery, digital transformation, and structural decarbonization, the design of financial systems will play a central role. Policymakers face critical trade-offs: how to expand access without compromising stability, how to leverage innovation without undermining regulation, and how to channel finance toward long-term development goals. Our findings offer evidence-based insights to inform such decisions.

Importantly, the study does not claim that finance always leads or follows growth. Rather, it argues that the finance–growth relationship in Asia is contingent, nonlinear, and mediated by structural and policy variables. Through meta-analysis, we aim to uncover empirically grounded patterns that can inform future research and policymaking. In doing so, we treat Asia not as a monolithic case but as a diverse region whose varied financial experiences offer lessons for other parts of the world.

1.2 Key Findings from Existing Literature

Over the past three decades, the finance–growth literature has shifted from a broad consensus to a field marked by increasing nuance and empirical divergence. While early theoretical and empirical works broadly supported the notion that financial development catalyzes economic growth by mobilizing savings, improving capital allocation, and fostering technological progress (Schumpeter, 1911; King & Levine, 1993), more recent evidence has become increasingly nuanced, context-specific, and often contradictory.

At the theoretical level, endogenous growth models—especially those developed by Romer (1986) and Lucas (1988)—reinforced the idea that well-functioning financial systems play a central role in sustaining long-run growth by influencing innovation, human capital formation, and total factor productivity. Financial institutions, in particular, help mitigate information asymmetry, manage risk, and reduce transaction costs, all of which are vital for productive investment (Mesagan et al., 2023).

However, empirical findings across countries and time periods show substantial heterogeneity. One of the key insights from the empirical literature is the conditional nature of the finance–growth relationship. In a cross-country context, Asteriou et al. (2024) demonstrate that while financial development supports growth under moderate financial depth, it exhibits diminishing and even negative returns once a threshold is exceeded. This finding echoes Arcand et al. (2015), who argue that "too much finance" can lead to inefficiencies such as misallocated credit and speculative bubbles.

Institutional quality often emerges as a decisive factor shaping the direction and magnitude of this relationship. Haini et al. (2023) show that strong legal institutions and regulatory frameworks are critical for ensuring that financial development translates into long-term growth. In countries with weak governance or corruption-prone systems, financial deepening can fuel rent-seeking or inequality rather than productive investment.

Evidence from Asia reinforces these global findings. In East Asia, mature financial systems like those in Japan and South Korea are often associated with low or even negative marginal gains from further financial deepening, partly due to high private debt burdens and financial market saturation. In contrast, South Asian economies such as India and Bangladesh have benefited more significantly from improvements in financial access and digital inclusion. India's UPI and Bangladesh's mobile finance ecosystem have facilitated rapid expansion in financial inclusion, especially among underserved populations (Demetriades et al., 2024).

Country-specific evidence further illuminates the complex dynamics at play. Mengesha and Berde (2023), examining Ethiopia, find that the finance–growth relationship is both nonlinear and asymmetric. Economic expansion appears to stimulate financial development more than financial sector growth drives economic output, particularly in low-income contexts. This calls into question the conventional assumption of finance as a principal driver of growth and instead supports a more reciprocal or growth-led finance model.

Financial structure also matters. Ye et al. (2023) argue that the alignment between financial architecture and technological capability is crucial for growth. In their study of Chinese provinces, regions with financial structures well-matched to the risk profiles of their dominant technologies (e.g., Chongqing) experienced stronger economic outcomes than those with mismatched systems (e.g., Hainan). This reinforces the notion that structural coherence between finance and real-sector dynamics is essential.

Institutional frameworks continue to be a recurrent theme in empirical analyses. Huo et al. (2023) emphasize the importance of governance, legal capacity, and policy credibility in shaping the efficacy of financial development. They argue that absence of institutional safeguards, financial liberalization may lead to macroeconomic instability, capital flight, or speculative cycles—rather than sustainable growth.

Globalization further complicates the finance–growth nexus. While access to global capital can improve financial efficiency and increase liquidity, it may also expose developing economies to external shocks and volatility. Haini et al. (2023) caution that financial openness without strong domestic institutions can crowd out domestic intermediation and dilute the growth benefits of finance.

In addition to institutional and globalization effects, the type of finance also matters. Asteriou et al. (2024) find that stock market development tends to produce more linear and robust growth benefits compared to bank-based systems, which often display threshold effects and are more prone to fragility in over-extended contexts. These findings have particular relevance for Asian economies seeking to rebalance toward capital market-led financial architectures to support innovation and long-term capital formation.

Taken together, the literature yields three consistent themes. First, financial development can support growth, but its effects are neither automatic nor universal. Second, the relationship is often nonlinear—beneficial up to a point but potentially detrimental beyond it. Third, contextual variables such as institutional quality, regulatory frameworks, and financial structure significantly condition outcomes.

For policymakers, these findings underscore the need for tailored financial strategies. One-size-fits-all models are increasingly obsolete. Financial deepening must be complemented by strong institutions, targeted regulation, and policies that align financial structures with the real economy. Particularly in Asia—where countries range from advanced economies with saturated markets to emerging ones with large unbanked populations—context-sensitive design is crucial.

This book builds upon these insights by offering a systematic, comparative, and methodologically rigorous meta-analysis of finance–growth linkages in Asia. Drawing on 759 effect-size estimates from 79 empirical studies, this study addresses key gaps in the literature, clarifying when, where, and how financial development promotes economic growth—and when it does not. By moving beyond country-level anecdotes toward a regionally integrated evidence base, it aims to advance both theory and policy in the evolving debate on finance and development.

1.3 Our Positioning: What This Book Adds

This book positions itself at the confluence of three maturing but still fragmented streams of economic research: the finance–growth literature, the political economy of globalization, and the use of meta-analytic techniques in development economics. While each of these domains has advanced significantly in recent years, their intersection remains underexplored—particularly in the context of Asia's highly diverse and institutionally differentiated economies. This book fills that gap, both by synthesizing the empirical literature and by developing a framework for understanding how financial development and globalization interact in shaping growth trajectories.

The finance–growth literature, now several decades deep, has generated extensive theoretical and empirical work on the channels through which financial systems influence macroeconomic performance. Much of this literature has focused on identifying average effects across countries or time periods, often emphasizing the positive role of credit intermediation, capital market development, and financial inclusion. Yet, as multiple reviews have shown (Levine, 2005; Beck, 2009), the results are far from uniform. Recent studies increasingly acknowledge the conditional nature of the finance–growth nexus—affected by institutions, policy sequencing, income levels, and external shocks. However, relatively few studies have examined the regional structure of these differences or modeled globalization as an endogenous part of the finance–growth relationship.

This book directly addresses that lacuna. Our primary contribution is to isolate and quantify the moderating role of globalization in the finance–growth nexus across Asian economies. Rather than treating globalization as a background condition or exogenous context, we model it explicitly using a set of operational proxies—including capital account openness, stock market liberalization, and trade integration. In doing so, we depart from studies that simply treat financial development as a unidirectional engine of growth, regardless of the external environment. The core insight here is that financial development and globalization are not parallel processes—they are co-evolving, and their interaction shapes how capital is allocated, regulated, and leveraged for growth.

A second critical contribution lies in our focus on regional heterogeneity. Most meta-analyses in this field adopt a global lens, aggregating findings across regions that differ profoundly in institutional structures, financial depth, and reform histories. This aggregation risks obscuring important subregional dynamics—particularly in Asia, where East and South Asia have followed divergent development paths. Our analysis disaggregates the literature accordingly, showing that South Asia consistently exhibits stronger growth payoffs from financial development than East Asia. The reasons for this are structural: South Asia's lower baseline levels of financial access and institutional maturity mean that even marginal improvements—such as digital financial inclusion or SME credit expansion—can have large effects. East Asia, by contrast, while home to more advanced financial systems, often displays signs of saturation, volatility, and diminishing marginal returns. This regional differentiation provides a more precise and policy-relevant account of how financial development operates in practice.

Methodologically, this book extends the application of meta-analysis in development economics by incorporating tools that have only recently gained traction. In addition to conventional fixed- and random-effects synthesis, we apply Bayesian Model Averaging (BMA) and Weighted-Average Least Squares (WALS) to address model uncertainty in the presence of many correlated moderators. We also apply weighted average of adequately powered (WAAP) estimators and a suite of techniques to detect and adjust for publication selection bias—including the Funnel Asymmetry

Test, Precision-Effect Test, and Precision-Effect Estimate with Standard Error (FAT–PET–PEESE) framework, the selection model, the endogenous kinked model, and p-uniform methods. These approaches allow us to go beyond averages and statistical significance to identify patterns that are robust, replicable, and economically meaningful. This level of methodological transparency is essential in a field where empirical results are often sensitive to study design, sample characteristics, and reporting conventions.

Beyond technical contribution, this book aims to generate applied value. Too often, the finance–growth literature stops short of informing policy, either due to conceptual ambiguity or methodological opacity. By structuring the empirical findings into region-specific narratives and stylized scenarios, we offer practical insights that can support policy design. These are not "silver bullets," but they do offer a typology of what works under what conditions. Whether it is sequencing liberalization behind regulatory readiness, promoting equity markets in emerging systems, or scaling digital financial infrastructure, the lessons distilled here are empirically grounded and regionally attuned.

In this way, the book contributes to a broader agenda: not only to update our understanding of financial development in Asia, but to reframe the finance–growth conversation in terms of credibility, conditionality, and institutional context. By anchoring its findings in both statistical synthesis and regional specificity, this book moves the debate beyond binary claims of "finance good" or "finance bad." Instead, it offers a data-rich framework for understanding how finance can work for development—when designed, sequenced, and governed effectively in a globalized world.

1.4 Advancements Beyond Prior Works

This book builds directly upon our earlier research—most notably, the 2023 article published in the Asian Development Review—while substantially extending its empirical depth, theoretical scope, and methodological precision. The prior study provided an initial quantitative synthesis of the finance–growth nexus in Asia, identifying broad patterns across a diverse set of national contexts. It established the presence of a positive, albeit heterogeneous, relationship between financial development and economic growth in the region. However, several limitations in that earlier work left important questions unresolved, particularly in relation to the roles of globalization, institutional context, and methodological design.

First, the present volume introduces a significantly expanded and updated dataset. Whereas the 2023 article was based on approximately 400 effect-size estimates, the book draws upon 759 estimates extracted from studies published through 2024. This near-doubling of the sample size allows for finer-grained meta-regressions and enables the detection of interaction effects that would have been statistically underpowered in the earlier work. The enlarged dataset not only strengthens the generalizability of the findings but also provides a firmer empirical foundation for analyzing sources of heterogeneity across countries, time periods, and estimation techniques.

Second, this book systematically adopts several advanced econometric techniques that were absent from the earlier article. These include WAAP estimates and BMA, both of which address limitations associated with small-sample bias and model uncertainty. These tools allow us to assess the robustness of our findings across competing specifications and to account for potential overfitting in the meta-regression models. Additionally, we incorporate a more rigorous suite of publication bias diagnostics—including PET-PEESE and selection models—which help disentangle genuine empirical effects from those potentially driven by selective reporting. This enhanced methodological toolkit represents a clear step forward in the rigor and transparency of our meta-analytic design.

Third, the current volume significantly deepens the theoretical integration of globalization into the finance–growth relationship. The 2023 article acknowledged globalization as a background factor but did not operationalize its moderating role. This book addresses that gap by embedding multiple proxies of globalization—both de jure and de facto financial openness—into the meta-regression framework. We systematically test whether globalization conditions the marginal effect of financial development on growth and find evidence that its impact is contingent on institutional quality and regional context. This represents a critical theoretical advance, allowing us to speak to the complex interplay between domestic financial systems and external economic integration.

Fourth, the book offers a full-length analysis of regional heterogeneity, with disaggregated results for South Asia and East Asia. This contrasts with the earlier article, where regional differentiation was only briefly discussed. By devoting a dedicated chapter to comparative regional analysis, we highlight how structural differences—such as the degree of state control, the maturity of financial markets, and exposure to financial crises—mediate the finance–growth relationship. For instance, we observe that digital financial inclusion in India, or macroprudential regulation in Korea, can significantly reshape the effectiveness of financial intermediation. This regional disaggregation yields insights that are essential for tailoring policy recommendations to specific subregional dynamics.

Finally, the book is conceived not only as a scholarly contribution but also as a practical resource for a wider audience. It includes pedagogical features such as executive summaries of each chapter, a glossary of key terms, stylized policy scenarios, and a set of methodological appendices. These additions are designed to make the volume more accessible to a broader audience, including graduate students, policymakers, and development practitioners. In doing so, the book aims to bridge the gap between academic research and applied decision-making, particularly in the context of financial sector development strategies across emerging Asian economies.

In sum, this book builds on the foundation laid by our earlier work but moves decisively beyond it. Through an expanded dataset, improved econometric techniques, deeper theoretical modeling, and sharper regional disaggregation, it provides a more comprehensive and policy-relevant account of the finance–growth nexus in Asia. These advancements allow us to generate new insights, challenge simplified narratives, and offer more targeted recommendations for fostering inclusive and resilient financial systems across the region.

1.5 Chapter Roadmap and Structure of the Book

The book is structured into seven core chapters and a supporting appendix, carefully designed to balance conceptual clarity, methodological rigor, and empirical depth. Each chapter builds progressively to guide the reader from theoretical grounding through analytical execution to practical insights, ensuring a coherent and engaging narrative. The aim is not merely to describe empirical patterns but to interrogate the underlying mechanisms and offer evidence-based conclusions relevant to both scholars and policymakers.

Chapter 1 introduces the motivation behind the study, situating the book within the broader academic and policy debates on finance, growth, and globalization in Asia. It outlines the rationale for a region-specific meta-analysis, particularly in light of Asia's institutional diversity and financial heterogeneity. This chapter also frames the key research questions and explains how the book contributes to ongoing conversations in development economics and international finance. In doing so, it positions the study at the intersection of empirical synthesis and regional economic analysis.

Chapter 2 lays the conceptual foundations of the book. It surveys the theoretical literature that links financial development with economic growth, integrating insights from endogenous growth theory, financial intermediation, and institutional economics. It also examines how globalization—through mechanisms like trade openness, capital mobility, and foreign investment—can shape or moderate this finance–growth nexus. The chapter concludes by presenting a set of testable hypotheses, organized around core theoretical expectations and contextual variations across Asia.

Chapter 3 turns to the empirical architecture of the study. It explains the construction of the meta-analytic dataset, including the systematic search strategy and inclusion criteria applied to select relevant empirical studies. This chapter also elaborates on the variable coding protocol and the operationalization of key concepts such as globalization and financial development. Special attention is given to emerging themes like digital finance and post-COVID recovery, which are integrated into the coding scheme to allow for exploratory analysis. The transparent and replicable design of the dataset reinforces the credibility of the findings.

Chapter 4 presents the book's methodological framework. It introduces the core tools of meta-regression analysis, outlining their applicability and limitations in synthesizing heterogeneous empirical results. The chapter discusses a range of estimators, including traditional random-effects models as well as more recent innovations such as BMA, WAAP estimates, and bias-correction methods like PET-PEESE. This methodological pluralism is necessary to address concerns around publication bias, small-sample inference, and model uncertainty.

Chapter 5 delivers the main empirical findings. It begins with the baseline estimates of the finance–growth relationship and then explores moderator effects, focusing especially on the role of globalization. The chapter also examines subregional patterns, contrasting findings across South Asia, East Asia, and other Asian subregions. To enhance policy relevance, the analysis is extended to include stylized policy scenarios, which illustrate how different levels of globalization and financial maturity can produce divergent growth outcomes.

Chapter 6 reinforces the robustness and reliability of the empirical results. It reports on a range of diagnostic checks, including publication bias tests, sensitivity analyses, and the use of alternative estimators. These robustness exercises ensure that the findings are not artifacts of model choice or sample selection but reflect consistent empirical patterns.

Chapter 7 synthesizes the book's conclusions and outlines key policy implications. It draws together the major findings and interprets them in light of current debates in economic development. The chapter offers differentiated recommendations for financial sector reform, globalization strategies, and institutional development across Asia. It also identifies avenues for future research, especially in light of digitalization, climate finance, and shifting global economic dynamics.

Finally, the Appendix serves as a technical companion to the main text. It includes the list of studies included in the meta-analysis, detailed notes on estimator implementation, and a comprehensive variable coding manual. Collectively, the book aims to provide a transparent, evidence-rich, and policy-relevant account of how finance and globalization jointly influence economic growth in Asia. To rigorously assess the patterns introduced in the preceding chapter and move beyond fragmented, case-specific insights, the next chapter lays out the conceptual and methodological foundations of the meta-regression framework.

CHAPTER 2

Conceptual Foundations—Finance, Globalization, and Development Policy

2.1 Theories of Finance–Growth Linkages

Theoretical perspectives on the finance–growth nexus have evolved significantly since the seminal insights of Schumpeter (1912), Gurley and Shaw (1955), and Goldsmith (1959), who each emphasized the catalytic role of financial systems in promoting innovation, mobilizing savings, reducing transaction costs, and efficiently allocating capital. These early theorists laid the foundation for the "supply-leading" hypothesis, which posits that financial development precedes and stimulates economic growth by fostering capital accumulation and technological progress. This viewpoint has been revisited and expanded by contemporary endogenous growth theorists, such as Romer (1986) and Lucas (1988), who underline how financial markets and institutions enhance total factor productivity through better allocation of resources and support for innovation-driven activities (Aghion et al., 2005).

In particular, financial systems reduce information asymmetries and agency costs, thereby facilitating risk pooling, credit allocation, and the governance of corporate behavior (Levine, 2003; Law et al., 2013). These functions channel resources towards high-yielding sectors and firms, thus reinforcing productive investment. Sound financial development also fosters entrepreneurial activity and technological diffusion, creating an endogenous loop of finance-induced growth (Ye et al., 2023).

A. Anwar, I. Iwasaki, *Meta-Analysis of Finance and Growth in Asia*,
https://doi.org/10.1007/978-3-032-10219-5_2

However, empirical research over the past two decades has cast doubt on a universally positive finance–growth relationship. A growing strand of literature has emphasized that financial development can become detrimental beyond a certain threshold—a phenomenon often described as an inverted U-shaped relationship. For instance, Arcand et al. (2015) and Asteriou and Spanos (2022) provide evidence that excessive credit expansion, particularly through the banking sector, can fuel financial fragility and misallocation of resources. This is particularly the case in the absence of robust institutions or during times of macroeconomic stress, such as the 2008–2009 global financial crisis or the COVID-19 pandemic (Demetriades et al., 2024).

Indeed, recent studies highlight that financial fragility—measured by impaired loan ratios, liquidity constraints, and weak bank capitalization—can weaken or reverse the growth benefits of finance (Demetriades et al., 2024). Shadow banking systems and unregulated financial intermediaries further complicate this dynamic. Isayev and Farooq (2024) demonstrate that in countries with high levels of shadow banking, the marginal benefits of financial development increase, suggesting that these parallel financial institutions may complement traditional banks in delivering credit and financial services—though they also pose systemic risks when not subject to appropriate regulation.

Another important theoretical extension involves the structural alignment between finance and technology. Ye et al. (2023) propose that the optimal financial structure—whether bank-based or market-based—depends on the technological risk profile of an economy. In low-risk, imitative industrial environments, bank-based finance may suffice. But for innovation-intensive sectors, market-based systems may be more appropriate, allowing firms to access equity financing under high uncertainty. This argument underscores the importance of structural matching between the financial architecture and the real economy.

Moreover, financial globalization adds a new layer of complexity. Theoretical models predict that openness to cross-border capital flows should facilitate capital reallocation to countries with high marginal returns (Solow, 1956), thereby supporting convergence. However, empirical results are mixed. While Wang et al. (2023) confirm that financial openness benefits medium- and low-income countries through increased capital stock and productivity, they also note that its effects are conditional on institutional quality and economic stability. In fact, excessive openness can expose economies to volatility and contagion risks unless mediated by strong governance and regulatory institutions (Haini et al., 2023).

Institutional quality thus emerges as a critical mediating variable. The finance–growth linkage is stronger and more sustainable in countries with sound regulatory frameworks, effective contract enforcement, and political stability. As shown by Haini (2023), Cooray (2012), and others, institutional development complements financial deepening by enhancing its efficiency and inclusiveness.

In sum, the finance–growth relationship operates through multiple, sometimes conflicting channels. At one end, financial systems support economic growth by reducing frictions and spurring investment and innovation. At the other, they can generate volatility, misallocation, and fragility when expansion is unchecked or unaccompanied by institutional safeguards. These theoretical insights help explain why the finance–growth nexus varies not only across countries and over time but also across financial structures, degrees of openness, and institutional contexts—issues that are explored further in subsequent sections of this chapter.

2.2 Globalization as a Conditional Amplifier

Globalization plays a complex, multifaceted role in moderating the finance–growth relationship. It amplifies the capacity of financial systems to influence growth trajectories, but this influence is neither uniform nor unconditional. The impact of globalization operates through trade openness, capital mobility, technological diffusion, and institutional convergence. Each channel can either reinforce or destabilize the finance–growth linkage, depending on a country's initial conditions, policy choices, and level of institutional maturity.

Theoretically, globalization enhances the allocative efficiency of financial markets by expanding access to international capital, enabling portfolio diversification, and incentivizing regulatory improvements. In a neoclassical framework, financial openness should facilitate capital inflows from capital-abundant to capital-scarce countries, leading to convergence in growth rates (Solow, 1956). Empirical studies such as Bekaert et al. (2005, 2011) confirm this mechanism, showing that liberalized equity markets in emerging economies improve capital accumulation and total factor productivity. These gains, however, are contingent on robust domestic institutions. Without them, globalization can amplify volatility and institutional weaknesses, resulting in financial crises and long-term economic scarring.

Asia presents a sharp dichotomy. East Asian economies—especially Japan, Korea, and China—have deeply integrated into global markets through export-led strategies and gradual capital account liberalization. Their experience illustrates how carefully sequenced globalization can support financial development and economic growth. China, for example, liberalized its trade regime well before opening its capital account, allowing it to harness the productivity gains of globalization while insulating its financial system from speculative pressures. This sequencing supported both financial deepening and macroeconomic stability, as reflected in sustained double-digit growth rates throughout the 2000s.

In contrast, South Asian countries have followed a more fragmented path. India's reforms in the early 1990s opened trade and capital flows, but these reforms were uneven and often implemented in response to external pressures or crises. As a result, India has experienced episodes of vulnerability—most notably the currency crisis of 1991 and capital outflow pressures during the 2013 taper tantrum. Despite these setbacks, globalization has enhanced India's access to foreign direct investment (FDI) and portfolio capital, supporting financial sector expansion and credit availability for productive sectors. However, the benefits have remained uneven due to institutional bottlenecks, regulatory opacity, and persistent informalization of the economy.

Recent empirical evidence underscores the conditional nature of globalization's effects. Wang et al. (2023) show that financial openness contributes positively to economic growth in medium- and low-income countries but has a negligible or even negative effect in high-income contexts. Their study disaggregates financial openness into de jure and de facto dimensions and finds that de jure liberalization—legal openness to capital flows—matters more in transitioning economies, where institutional frameworks are still evolving. Conversely, in more stable economies, de facto openness—actual cross-border flows—is a stronger driver. This distinction matters because it highlights that legal reforms without effective enforcement or absorptive capacity yield limited dividends.

Financial integration also interacts with institutional quality in nonlinear ways. Haini et al. (2023) demonstrate that the benefits of finance and institutions on growth are diminished at high levels of financial integration. Their threshold model reveals an inverted U-shaped relationship: up to a certain point, globalization strengthens the finance–growth nexus, but beyond that point, it introduces systemic risks that outweigh the gains.

These findings caution against the assumption that more integration is always better. Countries with fragile banking systems or shallow financial markets may be exposed to capital flight, exchange rate volatility, and procyclical capital flows, all of which destabilize long-term investment.

Globalization's influence also extends to financial structure. Ye et al. (2023) argue that the optimal financial structure depends on the technological complexity of the domestic economy. Market-based systems are more suited for economies with high innovation intensity, where risk tolerance and equity financing are essential. Conversely, bank-based systems work better in low-risk, imitation-driven sectors. Globalization can either reinforce or distort these patterns. For instance, countries that prematurely liberalize equity markets without the underlying demand from high-tech sectors may experience speculative bubbles rather than productive investment.

An equally important channel is institutional convergence. Globalization exerts pressure on countries to adopt international standards in banking regulation, corporate governance, and financial transparency. While this can promote institutional deepening, it can also lead to premature or superficial compliance. For example, several Southeast Asian economies adopted Basel accords under external pressure without adequate supervisory capacity, resulting in compliance gaps that were exposed during periods of financial stress.

FDI further illustrates globalization's moderating role. FDI can complement domestic financial development by introducing capital, technology, and managerial expertise. But its effects are spatially and institutionally heterogeneous. Petrakou et al. (2023) find that FDI has stronger growth effects in peripheral EU regions with less developed financial systems. This implies that globalization, via FDI, can compensate for financial underdevelopment when institutional support is adequate. In Asia, however, the distribution of FDI is highly skewed. Countries like Singapore, Hong Kong, and China absorb the majority of regional FDI, while others—such as Nepal or Bangladesh—struggle to attract consistent inflows due to political risk and infrastructure gaps.

Taken together, these insights suggest that globalization is not an exogenous shock to domestic finance but a dynamic and context-specific moderator. It can augment the finance–growth linkage where institutions are credible, sequencing is strategic, and financial systems are resilient. Conversely, it can undermine stability where financial openness exceeds absorptive capacity or where institutions are underdeveloped. Understanding globalization's moderating force thus requires moving beyond simplistic open-versus-closed paradigms of globalization and toward a more nuanced appreciation of country-specific trajectories, thresholds, and complementarities.

2.3 Institutions: The Architecture of Financial Effectiveness

The strength and structure of institutions are decisive in determining how financial development translates into sustained economic growth. Theoretically, institutions set the rules of the game—formal and informal—that govern market transactions, financial contracts, and the enforcement of property rights (North, 1990). Empirically, they influence how capital is allocated, how risks are managed, and how resources flow between productive and unproductive sectors. In the absence of strong institutional frameworks, financial development can become a source of volatility rather than a driver of growth.

The centrality of institutional quality to development outcomes is well-established in the empirical literature. Beck et al. (2003) argue that institutions that enforce property rights and uphold the rule of law are fundamental for finance to contribute positively to growth. Without these foundational structures, financial markets tend to misallocate credit toward politically connected firms or speculative activities, undermining allocative efficiency and productivity gains. Cooray (2012) reinforces this argument in the Asian context, showing that institutional quality not only enhances financial sector performance but also magnifies its growth effects.

Institutional quality operates along several dimensions. Legal systems that offer timely and impartial contract enforcement improve investor confidence and reduce credit risk. Regulatory bodies that ensure transparency, accountability, and compliance deter rent-seeking and corruption. Political stability and bureaucratic competence minimize policy uncertainty and foster long-term investment. These institutional features determine the extent to which financial resources support innovation, entrepreneurship, and structural transformation.

The role of institutions becomes even more critical in countries with nascent or rapidly liberalizing financial systems. In Asia, this is particularly evident. For example, Haini (2020) finds that in ASEAN economies, financial development alone does not yield significant growth dividends unless complemented by high institutional quality. Countries like Singapore and Malaysia, which have developed both robust legal systems and efficient regulatory environments, have been able to translate financial deepening into broad-based growth. In contrast, economies such as Myanmar or Laos, despite opening to foreign capital and expanding financial access, have not achieved comparable outcomes due to weak institutional foundations.

The relationship between institutions and finance is also interactive, not merely additive. Law et al. (2013) propose a "threshold hypothesis" in which financial development only becomes growth-enhancing once institutional quality surpasses a critical level. Their findings challenge the notion of linear causality and underscore the need for sequencing reforms. Premature liberalization of credit markets or capital accounts in weak institutional environments can exacerbate instability and entrench inequality. The Asian financial crisis of 1997–98 provides a textbook example: countries with similar levels of financial openness but differing institutional capacities experienced vastly different recovery trajectories.

Recent studies extend this line of inquiry by introducing nonlinearity into the finance–institution–growth nexus. Haini et al. (2023), using a global sample, identify a tipping point beyond which additional financial integration reduces the marginal benefit of both finance and institutions. Their evidence suggests that excessive financial openness, when not accompanied by institutional upgrading, may dilute or even reverse earlier gains. This underscores the importance of policy coordination between financial and institutional reforms.

The salience of institutional quality is further evident when comparing East and South Asia. East Asian economies such as Japan, Korea, and Taiwan developed strong bureaucratic and legal institutions alongside financial expansion, allowing for strategic industrial policy, efficient capital allocation, and technological upgrading. The result has been sustained growth, low inequality, and high levels of financial inclusion. South Asia presents a more mixed picture. India, despite having an independent judiciary and a reasonably competent central bank, suffers from regulatory bottlenecks, judicial delays, and fragmented enforcement mechanisms. As a result, financial development has not fully translated into equitable or consistent growth. Pakistan and Bangladesh face even more acute institutional deficits, where weak property rights and political instability limit the productivity of financial capital.

Institutional quality also influences the effectiveness of development finance. State-led financial institutions, such as development banks or housing finance corporations, play a crucial role in channeling credit to underserved sectors. But their performance varies widely depending on governance standards. For example, India's National Bank for Agriculture and Rural Development (NABARD) has successfully supported rural development due to relatively strong institutional oversight and performance metrics. In contrast, politically captured development finance institutions in other South Asian countries have often operated as conduits for patronage, leading to inefficiency and fiscal strain.

Moreover, institutional development is a necessary condition for harnessing foreign capital effectively. Anwar and Iwasaki (2023) find that the finance–growth nexus in Asia is significantly stronger in countries with stable legal and regulatory institutions. Their meta-analysis across 75 studies highlights how institutional quality mediates the absorption of FDI, the efficiency of credit markets, and the stability of capital flows. The implication is clear: financial development in the absence of institutional safeguards may lead to short-term gains but long-term fragility.

Finally, institutional credibility is central to public trust in financial systems. Financial inclusion strategies, fintech adoption, and market-based financing mechanisms all depend on public willingness to engage with formal finance. Where institutions are perceived as corrupt or biased, households and firms revert to informal networks, limiting the scale and effectiveness of financial development. Institutional reform, therefore, is not an adjunct to financial policy but a foundational pillar of development strategy.

In sum, institutional quality is not merely a background variable in the finance–growth story—it is the scaffolding on which the financial system rests. Without reliable institutions, financial deepening risks being diverted toward rent extraction or speculative bubbles. With strong institutions, finance can become a powerful catalyst for innovation, inclusion, and long-term development. As the Asian experience makes clear, the depth of finance must be matched by the depth of institutional capability to deliver durable growth outcomes.

2.4 Financial Liberalization, Inequality, and Developmental Trade-offs

Financial liberalization—typically involving the removal of interest rate controls, credit allocation restrictions, and capital account barriers—has long been promoted as a catalyst for economic growth and financial deepening. However, its implications for inequality and sustainable development remain deeply contested. While liberalization may enhance efficiency and access to capital, its distributional consequences are highly uneven. In many cases, rapid financial deregulation has exacerbated wealth gaps, distorted credit markets, and undermined progress toward the Sustainable Development Goals (SDGs), particularly in developing regions like Asia.

Theoretically, liberalized financial systems are expected to allocate capital more efficiently by responding to market signals rather than political mandates. They should encourage competition, improve savings mobilization, and increase access to credit. Yet, in practice, the gains from financial liberalization are not evenly distributed across social classes, sectors, or regions. The "trickle-down" logic embedded in liberalization reforms assumes that once capital markets are freed, the benefits will eventually reach low-income groups via greater employment, lower interest rates, or more inclusive financial services. This assumption, however, rarely holds in fragile institutional contexts or unequal societies.

A core issue lies in the asymmetry of access. Financial liberalization tends to favor those who are already integrated into formal financial systems—large firms, urban households, and foreign investors—while excluding informal enterprises, rural communities, and low-income groups. For instance, following India's financial sector reforms in the early 1990s, credit to large corporations and service-sector firms expanded rapidly, but rural credit shrank in relative terms. Small-scale farmers and microenterprises saw limited improvements in financial access, despite broader capital market growth. The same pattern has emerged in other liberalizing economies, including the Philippines and Indonesia, where commercial banks focused on high-margin lending to urban consumers and large corporates while sidelining the rural poor.

These dynamics have significant implications for inequality. Arestis and Caner (2009) find that financial liberalization tends to increase income inequality in developing countries, particularly where institutional safeguards are weak. Liberalization often leads to credit booms that disproportionately benefit asset owners, pushing up the value of equities and real estate and widening the gap between the rich and poor. This effect is amplified by financial volatility, which disproportionately harms low-income households with limited capacity to absorb shocks. Episodes such as the 1997–1998 Asian financial crisis and the 2008 global financial meltdown exposed how deregulated financial flows could rapidly reverse and destabilize entire economies, with the poorest bearing the brunt of the fallout.

Moreover, the design of financial liberalization programs often ignores local development needs. Liberalization tends to prioritize macroeconomic indicators—such as capital account openness and market efficiency—over sectoral or social outcomes. As a result, the financial system becomes geared toward short-term profit maximization rather than long-term investment in education, health, or green infrastructure. This is directly at odds with the goals of the 2030 Agenda for Sustainable Development, which requires financial systems to support inclusive, equitable, and environmentally sustainable growth.

The SDGs emphasize poverty reduction (SDG 1), reduced inequality (SDG 10), gender equality (SDG 5), and decent work (SDG 8), all of which require targeted financial flows. Yet liberalized markets tend to overlook these sectors due to their lower profit margins and higher perceived risks. For example, green investments, social enterprises, and women-led startups often struggle to access mainstream finance despite their alignment with the SDGs. Without active policy intervention, financial liberalization alone does not create the incentive structure necessary to support sustainable development.

Some economies have responded to this gap by promoting inclusive finance through targeted regulation and developmental institutions. Bangladesh's experience is illustrative. While its financial sector remains partially liberalized, the government has maintained a strong developmental mandate through institutions like Grameen Bank and Bangladesh Bank's refinancing schemes for microenterprises. These programs have significantly expanded credit access among low-income households, particularly women, contributing to measurable improvements in health, education, and rural livelihoods—key SDG indicators.

Similarly, China's cautious approach to capital account liberalization has allowed it to retain control over credit flows to priority sectors, including clean energy, affordable housing, and poverty alleviation. State-owned banks, guided by industrial policy, have financed large-scale infrastructure and social programs without succumbing to the volatility seen in more open financial regimes. While not without flaws, this model highlights how strategic sequencing and institutional coordination can mitigate the regressive tendencies of liberalized finance.

However, in many parts of South Asia and Southeast Asia, the move toward liberalization has not been paired with adequate redistribution mechanisms. Social safety nets remain underdeveloped, financial literacy is low, and credit rating systems exclude large sections of the population. This institutional vacuum enables a dual-track financial system—sophisticated for privileged groups, exclusionary for broader populations. Consequently, inequality persists or worsens, even as headline indicators of financial deepening improve.

To align financial liberalization with the SDGs, countries must embed inclusion, resilience, and sustainability into their financial governance frameworks. This includes enforcing regulations that direct credit to underserved sectors, incentivizing banks to serve low-income borrowers, strengthening financial education, and integrating ESG (environmental, social, and governance) criteria into lending practices. It also means building institutions that can mediate between financial markets and social priorities—development banks, impact investment platforms, and fintech solutions designed for financial inclusion.

In sum, while financial liberalization may expand the size and scope of financial markets, it does not inherently promote equitable or sustainable outcomes. Left unchecked, it risks entrenching privilege, amplifying volatility, and sidelining the development needs of marginalized populations. If liberalization is to contribute meaningfully to the SDGs, it must be carefully designed, sequenced, and governed—not as an end in itself, but as a tool for broader societal transformation.

2.5 Regional Divergence in Asia and the Formulation of Hypotheses

The finance–growth nexus in Asia does not follow a uniform pattern. Rather, it reveals a landscape shaped by distinct reform trajectories, uneven institutional development, and varied responses to globalization. While foundational theories by Schumpeter (1912), Gurley and Shaw (1955), and Goldsmith (1959) have argued that financial development spurs growth by mobilizing savings, enhancing resource allocation, and reducing transaction costs, the empirical reality across Asia underscores substantial regional variation. These disparities, particularly between East and South Asia, demand closer examination as they inform our understanding of how financial systems support, constrain, or transform growth trajectories in differing contexts.

Much of East Asia embarked on financial liberalization and institutional reform relatively early. Countries such as Japan, Korea, and later China initiated reforms in the 1970s and 1980s, combining export-led industrialization with gradual financial market development. In contrast, South Asian countries—India, Bangladesh, Pakistan, and Nepal—pursued more delayed and fragmented reform paths, with most financial sector deregulation and institutional modernization occurring only in the 1990s. This difference in the timing and sequencing of reforms has influenced both the pace and quality of financial deepening in each subregion (Anwar & Sun, 2011).

The 1997 Asian Financial Crisis further differentiated the regions. East and Southeast Asian economies were more severely affected, exposing the fragility of liberalized but under-regulated capital markets. In contrast, most South Asian countries, being less financially integrated, were insulated from the worst contagion effects (Anwar & Cooray, 2012). This divergence not only underscored the risks of premature liberalization without robust institutional scaffolding but also demonstrated that financial openness alone does not guarantee resilience or sustainable growth.

A key differentiator lies in institutional development. In East Asia, institutional reforms—such as improvements in regulatory quality, judicial efficiency, and governance transparency—have often complemented financial liberalization. Countries like Korea and Singapore built robust oversight mechanisms, independent central banks, and effective commercial courts to accompany market reforms. These institutional investments facilitated productive credit allocation, curbed systemic risk, and encouraged long-term investment. In contrast, institutional upgrading in South Asia has been uneven. Haini (2020) shows that in ASEAN countries, the impact of financial development on growth is contingent on the quality of institutions. The same holds for South Asia, where weak enforcement, political instability, and corruption often dilute the growth-enhancing effects of finance.

The contrast between China and India illustrates these dynamics vividly. China's state-led financial deepening has been anchored in strong bureaucratic structures, strategic capital allocation, and tightly sequenced reforms. Despite retaining elements of financial repression, China has effectively leveraged finance for industrial and infrastructural transformation. India's more liberalized financial system, on the other hand, has struggled with regulatory fragmentation, nonperforming assets, and insufficient credit to SMEs. While both countries have attracted substantial FDI, China's success has been more evenly distributed across regions and sectors due to tighter institutional coordination and a clearer policy direction (Anwar & Cooray, 2012; Anwar & Iwasaki, 2023).

This leads to the first hypothesis:

Hypothesis 1 The impact of financial development and liberalization on economic growth in Asia is positive and economically meaningful.

This hypothesis stems from the theoretical assumption that financial development reduces intermediation costs, increases credit availability, and facilitates investment and innovation. Empirical studies—such as those by Levine (2003) and Law et al. (2013)—support this, showing that deeper financial systems are associated with higher GDP growth. Aghion et al. (2005) extend this argument by noting that finance supports innovation by reducing screening costs and agency problems. Yet, these benefits are not automatic and are highly conditional on institutional and structural readiness.

The second key variation across Asia lies in the interaction between financial development, foreign capital, and macroeconomic convergence. Anwar and Iwasaki (2023) find that FDI and financial openness yield stronger growth dividends in countries with higher institutional capacity. This finding is especially relevant in Asia, where the distribution of foreign investment is starkly unequal. East Asia—particularly China, Hong Kong, and Japan—has captured the bulk of FDI inflows, supported by stable macroeconomic environments, infrastructure readiness, and policy coherence. In contrast, South Asia's FDI landscape is highly concentrated in India, with countries like Pakistan, Nepal, and Bangladesh attracting far less due to political uncertainty and regulatory unpredictability (Anwar & Sun, 2011).

Financial deepening also varies significantly across regions. According to Sharma and Kautish (2020), the ratio of private sector credit to GDP in South Asia was, until the 1990s, less than half that of high-income East Asian countries. This disparity reflects not only institutional constraints but also the depth of capital markets, financial literacy, and bank outreach.

While East Asia boasts more sophisticated bond and equity markets, much of South Asia remains heavily dependent on banking systems that often prioritize large borrowers and overlook rural and informal sectors. This structural bias limits finance's developmental potential and reinforces existing inequalities.

Despite these constraints, there are signs of improvement. Recent policy initiatives in South Asia—including microfinance expansion, rural banking programs, and fintech solutions—are beginning to address financial inclusion gaps. Government-backed financial institutions, such as housing finance corporations in India, Pakistan, and Bangladesh, have shown positive and statistically significant impacts on growth by targeting underserved populations (Nazir et al., 2021). However, these successes remain patchy and often depend on sustained political commitment and institutional follow-through.

Another distinguishing factor is macroeconomic resilience. Over the past two decades, many South Asian economies have stabilized inflation, improved fiscal management, and increased external buffers. This macroprudential strengthening has enhanced their capacity to absorb financial shocks and pursue gradual liberalization. Indeed, South Asia's relative immunity during the 1997 crisis and the 2008 global recession reflects a cautious approach to capital account liberalization and a more domestically anchored financial system (Ben Gamra, 2009; Sahoo, 2014).

Nonetheless, the theory of convergence suggests that capital-scarce countries—often lower-income—should experience higher returns to investment and faster growth. Aiyar (2001) argues that low capital–labor ratios in transitioning economies can yield superior marginal productivity of capital, providing a natural catch-up mechanism. If financial systems in such countries can effectively channel savings into high-return projects, growth convergence becomes achievable. However, the prerequisite is that financial development is accompanied by credible institutions and sound policy frameworks.

Global economic integration adds another layer of variation. East Asian countries, led by Japan, Korea, and China, are deeply embedded in global value chains, with open capital accounts and high trade-to-GDP ratios. This integration enhances their financial sector's responsiveness to global credit conditions and investment flows. South Asia, in contrast, remains more inward-looking, with lower trade openness and limited participation in global financial markets (Häusler, 2002; Porter, 2005). This gap affects the elasticity of finance-led growth and helps explain the subregional divergence in financial sector impact. These regional asymmetries ground the second hypothesis. While this may appear counterintuitive—given East Asia's more advanced financial systems—it reflects the higher marginal returns to financial access in less developed contexts. In South Asia, even incremental improvements in financial inclusion can unlock substantial growth potential, particularly where large segments of the population remain underserved and latent demand for credit and savings remains untapped.

Hypothesis 2 The finance–growth nexus in South Asia is stronger than that in East Asia.

This hypothesis appears counterintuitive, yet it rests on the idea of marginal returns and diminishing gains. Since East Asia has already attained relatively high levels of financial development, additional financial deepening may yield lower developmental returns. In contrast, South Asia, with its lower financial base and improving macroeconomic fundamentals, may benefit more from incremental reforms and expanding financial inclusion. The "better finance, more growth" proposition (Law et al., 2013) underscores that institutional readiness—not financial scale alone—determines the magnitude of finance's contribution to growth.

In sum, Asia's financial development story is not homogenous but differentiated by timing, institutions, capital openness, and integration. Recognizing these variations is essential to interpreting empirical patterns and designing context-sensitive financial sector reforms. The hypotheses outlined here serve as a foundation for the meta-analysis that follows, which aims to quantify and explain the heterogeneity in finance-led growth across Asia.

2.6 Conceptual Takeaways and Policy Anchors

The finance–growth nexus remains a central concern in development economics, not merely for its theoretical elegance but for its direct implications on economic policy across diverse institutional landscapes. The Asian context, characterized by divergent reform histories and developmental priorities, offers a compelling ground to revisit the conceptual foundations of this relationship. While the literature consistently supports the idea that financial development—through greater liquidity, efficient resource allocation, and innovation incentives—facilitates economic growth (Schumpeter, 1912;

Levine, 2003; Aghion et al., 2005), the Asian experience underscores that outcomes are not automatic but institutionally and regionally contingent.

From a policy perspective, one of the clearest takeaways is that financial development and liberalization must be sequenced and embedded within institutional upgrading. As observed in East Asia, early and coordinated reforms in financial and administrative institutions enabled Japan, Korea, and later China to leverage finance for structural transformation. Regulatory improvements, judicial reforms, and macroeconomic stability provided the scaffolding for credit to flow into high-productivity sectors and strategic investments. In this setting, the "better finance, more growth" proposition (Law et al., 2013) holds: financial liberalization, when backed by sound institutions, delivers sustained growth outcomes.

Contrast this with the more staggered and uneven liberalization paths in South Asia. India, Pakistan, Bangladesh, and others implemented financial reforms in the 1990s, but institutional constraints—such as weak enforcement mechanisms, regulatory fragmentation, and persistent political volatility—limited the depth and reach of these reforms. Yet, the policy relevance lies not in the underperformance of liberalization per se, but in the learning it offers: financial sector reforms must go hand in hand with the rule of law, regulatory clarity, and capable oversight to prevent elite capture and credit misallocation.

The attraction of FDI further illustrates the relevance of institutional quality. In East Asia, FDI surged due to investor confidence in stable regulatory regimes and macroeconomic fundamentals. Countries such as China and Singapore actively directed FDI into infrastructure, manufacturing, and technology, aligning external finance with development priorities. In South Asia, by contrast, FDI has been far more concentrated in India, while other countries continue to struggle with low inflows due to institutional fragility and limited investor protection (Anwar & Sun, 2011; Anwar & Cooray, 2012).

This divergence underscores an important policy implication: financial development amplifies the benefits of FDI only when institutions can absorb, channel, and monitor capital effectively. Without such capacity, FDI remains constrained or becomes concentrated in speculative or enclave sectors with limited spillovers. Moreover, the uneven distribution of FDI across and within regions reflects broader issues of governance, infrastructure readiness, and regulatory transparency—factors deeply embedded in institutional frameworks.

Another conceptual insight lies in the convergence hypothesis. Countries with low capital–labor ratios theoretically stand to gain higher returns from investment, but only if their financial systems are equipped to mobilize and allocate capital productively (Aiyar, 2001). This becomes a sharp policy challenge in many South Asian economies where low levels of financial deepening persist. As noted by Sharma and Kautish (2020), bank credit to the private sector in countries like India, Pakistan, and Bangladesh remained significantly below regional and global benchmarks well into the 1990s. Policymakers must therefore prioritize financial inclusion, rural banking infrastructure, and SME financing—not as ancillary policies, but as core components of growth strategy.

Encouragingly, targeted interventions such as public development banks, credit guarantee schemes, and housing finance corporations have shown positive impacts on growth across South Asia (Nazir et al., 2021). These findings suggest that even in institutionally weaker settings, carefully designed policy instruments can enhance the developmental role of finance. However, scaling these efforts requires strong fiscal governance and accountability frameworks, lest they devolve into channels of rent-seeking or political patronage.

The relative resilience of South Asian economies during the 1997 Asian Financial Crisis also reveals a counterpoint often overlooked in policy discourse. Their less open capital accounts and domestically anchored financial systems acted as buffers against external shocks. While this does not advocate financial autarky, it does suggest that gradualism in liberalization, paired with institutional strengthening, can offer a more stable development path than aggressive deregulation. South Asia's subsequent reforms—including the expansion of rural credit, financial technology (fintech), and microfinance—have increasingly emphasized inclusion and risk mitigation.

Still, East Asia's superior integration into global finance and trade markets—particularly in China, Korea, and Japan—has created additional growth channels through which financial development supports economic upgrading. The implication is that globalization interacts with finance in enabling, but also disciplining, ways. For instance, open capital accounts impose constraints on monetary and fiscal policy autonomy, making the need for strong institutions and macro-prudential oversight even more pressing (Häusler, 2002; Porter, 2005). Policymakers must therefore balance openness with regulatory capacity, ensuring that the domestic financial system remains resilient, inclusive, and aligned with development objectives.

Taken together, the conceptual takeaways from Asia are not only regionally instructive but globally relevant. They reinforce the view that financial development is not a technical or sectoral reform—it is a political and institutional process. Liberalization without governance invites instability. Inclusion without depth yields marginal gains. Stability without innovation leads to stagnation. The challenge for policymakers is to navigate these trade-offs with strategic intent, tailoring reforms to national contexts while anchoring them in institutional frameworks that ensure transparency, accountability, and developmental coherence.

In sum, the Asian experience affirms that financial development matters for growth—but how it matters depends critically on when, where, and through what institutions it is pursued. For South and East Asia alike, the policy priority should not merely be more finance, but better finance: finance that is transparent, inclusive, accountable, and strategically aligned with national development goals. These insights not only ground the hypotheses of this study but also set the stage for a rigorous empirical test of Asia's finance–growth relationship in the chapters that follow.

CHAPTER 3

Mapping the Literature—Scope, Dataset, and Study Selection

3.1 Systematic Search Strategy and PRISMA Approach

To compile a robust and policy-relevant dataset for this meta-analysis, we undertook a systematic literature search designed to identify empirical studies that examine the relationship between financial development, liberalization, and economic growth in the Asian context. Our search followed the Preferred Reporting Items for Systematic Reviews and Meta-Analyses (PRISMA) framework to ensure transparency and replicability in study selection and screening. We relied on two primary sources: the EconLit database and selected academic press websites affiliated with major economics and development journals.[1]

Using a Boolean "AND" search logic, we filtered papers whose titles contained at least one of the terms "finance" or "financial" in combination with "growth." This approach yielded an initial pool of approximately 3400 records from EconLit and an additional 730 entries from academic press websites. To ensure thematic relevance, we manually screened each title and abstract to identify studies that focused on Asian economies—either individual countries or regional groupings—and that provided empirical estimates of the finance–growth nexus.

We adopted four core inclusion criteria to refine the sample. First, studies had to be written in English. While this may introduce a degree of language bias, it allows for consistent screening and verification of results, particularly

A. Anwar, I. Iwasaki, *Meta-Analysis of Finance and Growth in Asia*,
https://doi.org/10.1007/978-3-032-10219-5_3

where multiple coders are involved in extracting statistical information. Second, only studies that report econometric estimates relevant to our analysis were retained. Specifically, we required sufficient information to derive or directly observe the associated t-statistic and degrees of freedom for at least one estimate of the finance–growth relationship. This criterion is essential for computing partial correlation coefficients (PCCs), which serve as the standardized effect size in our meta-regression models.

Third, we included both peer-reviewed journal articles and unpublished working papers. While one might question the inclusion of unpublished research, a growing body of meta-analytic literature encourages their use. Stanley and Doucouliagos (2012) argue that unpublished studies often address novel research questions, use more recent data, and adopt updated methodologies. Excluding them could lead to publication selection bias and weaken the representativeness of our findings. To avoid duplication and ensure quality, we retained only the final peer-reviewed version when a working paper had been subsequently published.

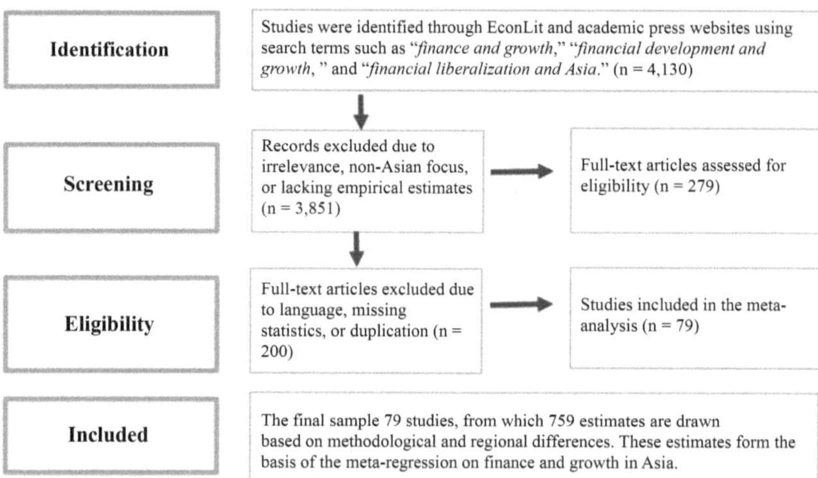

Fig. 3.1 PRISMA diagram of the literature search and study selection. Note The literature search and selection process follow the Preferred Reporting Items for Systematic Reviews and Meta-Analyses (PRISMA) guidelines, which provide a standardized framework for conducting and reporting meta-analyses. For a detailed discussion of PRISMA and best practices in meta-analytic research, see Havranek et al. (2020)

Finally, we applied a consistent coding protocol to ensure the comparability of extracted estimates across studies. This structured search and selection process underpins the empirical rigor of the meta-analysis and lays the foundation for identifying patterns of methodological heterogeneity and regional variation in Asia's finance–growth nexus.

The overall search and screening procedure is visually summarized in Fig. 3.1, which follows the PRISMA framework to illustrate the identification, screening, eligibility assessment, and final inclusion of studies. This diagram traces the flow of studies from initial identification through screening and eligibility assessment to final inclusion. From a total of 4130 records, 79 studies met all inclusion criteria and were retained for meta-analysis, yielding 759 estimates. The use of PRISMA ensures transparency, replicability, and methodological rigor in constructing the meta-analytic dataset.

3.2 Inclusion Criteria and Coding Protocol

The application of the inclusion criteria resulted in 79 eligible studies.[2] For this meta-analysis, we adopted a flexible coding protocol that permitted the extraction of multiple estimates from each study, provided they differed meaningfully in empirical approach, model specification, or analytical focus. This strategy acknowledges that the finance–growth nexus has been studied using varied designs and that these methodological differences can themselves be sources of heterogeneity worthy of systematic examination.

Table 3.1 provides a clear overview of the regional distribution and scope of the selected studies. Of the 79 studies, 8 examine Asia as a whole, 29 focus on East Asia, and 46 address South Asia, with 4 studies spanning both subregions. The temporal coverage is similarly broad: the included works span 72 years, from 1950 through 2021, capturing both early contributions to the finance–growth debate and recent empirical advances. Notably, 36 studies were published between 2015 and 2023, reflecting the growing academic interest in the region's financial transformations over the past decade.

Within this corpus, the operationalization of financial development and liberalization reflects substantial conceptual diversity. Building on the pioneering frameworks proposed by Beck et al. (2000) and Levine et al. (2000),

Table 3.1 Overview of collected estimates

Study type	*Number of studies*[a]	*Estimation period covered*	*Number of collected estimates (K)*	*Average number of estimates per study*	*Median number of estimates per study*
All studies	79	1950–2021	759	9.6	4
Studies of the whole of Asia	8	1975–2017	160	20.0	5
Studies of East Asia	29	1950–2021	332	11.4	6
Studies of South Asia[b]	46	1950–2018	267	5.8	4

Notes
[a] Four studies provide estimates both for East Asia and South Asia
[b] Includes Inner Asia

the studies employ a range of nine financial development indicators: financial depth, private credit to GDP, bank credit to GDP, private credit to domestic credit, market capitalization, stock market activity, turnover ratios, comprehensive financial development indexes, and other composite metrics. In addition, five indicators are commonly used to capture financial liberalization: capital account openness, financial market liberalization, stock market liberalization, comprehensive liberalization indexes, and related alternative measures.

The mean number of estimates per study is 9.6, with a median of 4, underscoring both the analytical richness and variability of the literature. The resulting dataset provides the necessary granularity to explore not only the average effects of finance on growth but also how these effects differ systematically across time periods, geographies, and methodological choices.

In sum, this structured inclusion and coding process creates a robust empirical foundation for the meta-analysis that follows, while also enabling an investigation into the sources of variation that underlie the finance–growth relationship in Asia.

3.3 Operationalizing Globalization and Emerging Themes

Globalization, as discussed in earlier chapters, is not a monolithic driver but a complex set of processes shaping the finance–growth relationship in Asia through multiple channels—trade, capital flows, technology diffusion, labor mobility, and institutional convergence. Understanding how globalization influences financial development requires more than acknowledging its presence; it demands a clear operationalization of its components and a nuanced appreciation of how these components manifest across different national and developmental contexts.

In the empirical literature, globalization has been approached not as a single variable but as a multidimensional construct captured through a variety of measurable proxies. This diversity reflects the reality that globalization operates through distinct yet overlapping mechanisms. Indicators such as trade openness, capital account liberalization, and foreign direct investment are widely used to represent economic globalization, while broader indices attempt to incorporate political and informational dimensions. Each of these indicators provides a different lens on how external integration shapes financial institutions, instruments, and outcomes.

Trade openness, for instance, remains a foundational proxy. It captures a country's integration into global goods and services markets, and by extension, the scale and complexity of its financial needs. As outlined in Chap. 1, trade liberalization stimulates the demand for financial services by increasing the volume of international transactions, creating exposure to foreign exchange volatility, and expanding the scope of firm-level financing requirements. In Asia, these dynamics have often been sector-specific—export credit systems in Bangladesh's garment sector, trade finance instruments in China post-WTO accession, and SME lending programs in Vietnam all reflect how trade openness can drive tailored financial development responses.

Capital account openness and financial liberalization indicators offer another window into globalization's impact. These proxies are particularly salient for middle-and high-income economies that have opened their financial systems to cross-border investment. Measures such as levels of FDI inflows, portfolio investments, and IMF de jure liberalization scores track the extent to which domestic capital markets are exposed to global financial cycles. These forms of openness have historically served as catalysts for financial sophistication, encouraging the development of capital markets, improving corporate governance standards, and attracting foreign expertise. Yet they also introduce volatility and policy risk, especially when liberalization outpaces regulatory capacity—as seen during the 1997 Asian Financial Crisis or the taper tantrum of 2013.

Beyond discrete indicators, the literature increasingly relies on composite indices to capture globalization's systemic character. Comprehensive metrics—such as the KOF Globalization Index or combined trade-finance openness scores—seek to measure the broader exposure of national economies to global forces. These indices blend economic, informational, and political dimensions, offering a holistic view of globalization's reach. However, they also raise methodological concerns, including aggregation bias and endogeneity, which must be accounted for in empirical analysis. Their growing use reflects a conceptual shift: globalization is no longer seen as a narrow economic phenomenon, but as a pervasive influence embedded in institutions, policy frameworks, and social structures.

Technological globalization constitutes another emerging theme. As highlighted in Chap. 1, the cross-border flow of digital infrastructure, software platforms, and innovation models has redefined how financial systems operate, especially in Asia's digitally ambitious economies. Indicators such as mobile subscription density, internet penetration rates, and digital transaction volumes are increasingly incorporated into empirical work to proxy for this less tangible but highly consequential form of globalization. In economies like India and China, technological globalization has not merely supplemented traditional finance—it has restructured it, producing new channels for inclusion, new forms of creditworthiness, and new modes of regulation.

Lastly, regional differentiation remains an essential axis along which globalization's financial consequences are interpreted. As elaborated in Chap. 1, South Asia and East Asia offer divergent models of globalization-mediated financial development. In South Asia, the relatively low baseline of financial inclusion means that even moderate increases in globalization—whether through trade, remittances, or digital platforms—can have transformative effects. In East Asia, where financial systems are already mature and highly integrated, the gains from further globalization are more conditional, often depending on institutional innovation, macroprudential vigilance, and demographic shifts.

Taken together, these themes underscore the complexity of operationalizing globalization in empirical research. No single indicator can adequately capture its multifaceted effects. Instead, a layered approach—sensitive to geography, development stage, institutional readiness, and policy sequencing—is needed. Understanding globalization as a set of interlocking processes, rather than a singular force, allows for a more realistic interpretation of its role in shaping Asia's financial evolution.

3.4 A Note on Effect Size Transformation: Partial Correlation Coefficient (PCC)

The empirical literature on globalization and financial development in Asia is marked by a rich diversity of analytical approaches. Scholars have employed a variety of functional forms—log-linear, log-log, semi-log, quadratic specifications, interaction terms, and more—to capture the nuanced ways in which global economic integration interacts with financial systems. While this methodological diversity reflects the complexity of the topic, it also presents a challenge for comparative synthesis. The coefficients reported in primary studies are often not directly comparable, owing to differences in scale, functional transformation, and underlying model structure. In short, the same relationship is being estimated across studies, but in structurally different ways (Stanley & Doucouliagos, 2012; Iwasaki, 2020a).

To address this challenge and facilitate meaningful comparison, this study employs the PCC as a common effect size metric. The PCC is a standardized measure that captures the strength and direction of association between two variables of interest—in this case, financial development and a globalization-related construct—while holding constant the influence of other covariates included in the original regression model. It is unit-free and bounded between − 1 and + 1, which allows for a consistent basis of comparison across studies, regardless of the functional form or the scale of the original variables (Hunter & Schmidt, 2004; Doucouliagos, 2005).

In adopting the PCC, the goal is not to oversimplify or flatten the conceptual richness of the primary literature. Rather, it is to ensure that the diversity of empirical strategies is preserved, while still enabling a form of aggregation that respects statistical comparability. This approach allows the synthesis to remain inclusive—embracing studies that vary in their estimation techniques, sample periods, and control structures—while placing them on a common analytical footing. Without such a transformation, the meta-analytical framework would be unable to provide coherent summary patterns or support downstream statistical procedures such as meta-regression (Stanley et al., 2013).

The use of PCC also aligns with broader conventions in the meta-analysis of economic relationships. In areas such as the finance–growth nexus, foreign aid effectiveness, and institutional quality, researchers have increasingly turned to standardized effect sizes to manage heterogeneity in model specifications (de Dominicis et al., 2008; Doucouliagos & Paldam, 2009; Iwasaki & Tokunaga, 2016). What makes the PCC particularly suitable in the present context is its ability to reflect the partial nature of the relationship—that is, to account for the fact that most primary studies do not examine globalization and financial development in isolation, but in the presence of multiple controls, fixed effects, and interaction terms. The PCC is therefore not simply a correlation coefficient in the traditional sense; it is a refined estimate that acknowledges the multivariate context in which financial development is usually studied.

It is worth noting that the transformation to PCC is applied consistently across all included estimates, using t-statistics and degrees of freedom reported in the original studies. This ensures that the meta-analytic database rests on transparent and reproducible foundations. Estimates for which sufficient statistical information was not available were excluded from the quantitative synthesis to maintain the integrity of the dataset. In line with best practices in research transparency, all transformation procedures and coding decisions are documented in the replication materials accompanying this volume.

For readers unfamiliar with the PCC or the rationale behind its calculation, it may be helpful to think of it as a translation device. Just as economists use purchasing power parity to compare incomes across countries with different currencies, the PCC allows researchers to compare effect sizes across studies with different model specifications. This transformation does not strip away the underlying theoretical or empirical complexity of the original research. Rather, it enables that complexity to be viewed and analyzed systematically.

A more detailed treatment of the PCC—including its statistical properties, limitations, and integration into meta-regression estimation—is provided in Chap. 4. There, the discussion turns to methodological choices, estimation techniques, and robustness considerations that build upon the foundations laid in this chapter.

3.5 Dataset Scope: Coverage and Quality

The meta-analysis presented in this volume draws upon a dataset designed to be as comprehensive, transparent, and policy-relevant as possible. As summarized earlier in Table 3.1, the sample includes studies covering all major Asian subregions, which offers a balanced basis for comparative meta-analysis and enables the examination of regional variation in the finance–growth nexus.

Studies were retained if they met four core eligibility criteria: (i) they were published in English; (ii) they focused empirically on at least one Asian economy or subregion; (iii) they reported quantitative estimates with sufficient information to derive standardized effect sizes; and (iv) they employed econometric approaches suitable for isolating the marginal effects of financial development or liberalization. Consistent with best practice recommendations (Stanley & Doucouliagos, 2012; Stanley, 2008), both peer-reviewed publications and unpublished working papers were included in order to mitigate the risk of publication selection bias and ensure that more recent empirical contributions were not overlooked.

The dataset demonstrates substantial methodological and thematic breadth. Across the studies, researchers have adopted diverse functional forms—log-linear, log-log, semi-log, quadratic—as well as a variety of estimators including OLS, GMM, and panel GLS. Data structures range from cross-sectional to panel and time series designs. This heterogeneity reflects the complexity of the topic and the adaptive strategies of scholars working across distinct country contexts and research questions.

All extracted estimates were transformed into PCCs to enable unit-free comparability, as explained in Sect. 3.4. This transformation ensures that differences in model specification and scaling do not preclude systematic synthesis.

To promote rigor and reproducibility, all coding decisions were cross-verified by the authors. Estimates that lacked the necessary statistical information (t-statistics, degrees of freedom) or were found to duplicate published versions were excluded. The result is a dataset of 759 effect sizes, combining depth and diversity, thus enabling a more nuanced and statistically robust exploration.[3]

Descriptive statistics of the collected estimates, including central tendency, dispersion, and distributional characteristics, are examined in detail in Sect. 3.6. For transparency, further documentation—such as the coding protocol, definitions of all moderator variables, and detailed references—is provided in the replication archive accompanying this volume.

3.6 Summary Table of Meta-Analyses

Before turning to multivariate meta-regression, it is essential to understand the statistical contours of the dataset. Table 3.2 presents a descriptive summary of the PCCs, offering the first quantitative window into the shape of the empirical literature on finance and growth in Asia. To complement these statistics, Fig. 3.2 illustrates the kernel density estimations of the collected estimates, providing an intuitive visual guide to their distribution.

The full sample comprises 759 effect sizes, with a mean PCC of 0.135 and a median of 0.163—suggesting that, on average, financial development and liberalization are positively associated with economic growth The standard deviation of 0.313 points to substantial variability, with estimates ranging from almost perfectly negative (–0.910) to strongly positive (0.896). The distribution shows moderate kurtosis (3.177) and a slight left skew (–0.227), highlighting the need to account for outliers and asymmetries.

Figure 3.2 visualizes this distribution, showing a pronounced concentration of estimates between 0.1 and 0.3, reinforcing the evidence for a broadly positive finance–growth link. The *t*-test confirms that the mean is statistically different from zero at the 1% level, supporting Hypothesis 1. Disaggregating by region uncovers clear contrasts. Studies focusing on South Asia (267 estimates) report a higher average PCC (0.177) and median (0.201), while studies of East Asia (332 estimates) yield more modest values (mean 0.062, median 0.072). Studies examining Asia as a whole display the highest average effect (0.218). These patterns suggest regional differences in the finance–growth relationship, which will be formally tested in Chap. 5.

Figure 3.2 provides further insight. The South Asian distribution (green dashed line) is sharply skewed to the right, reflecting a clustering of more strongly positive estimates. The East Asian distribution (red dashed line) is flatter and spreads more evenly around zero, indicating a higher frequency of small or negative effects. The line for studies of the whole of Asia (orange) peaks around 0.25, consistent with the higher mean.

Additional diagnostic tests bolster these observations. The Shapiro–Wilk normality test rejects the assumption of normal distribution for all subsamples except East Asia, suggesting that the variance in reported effects is not merely random noise but reflects underlying structural or methodological differences.

Table 3.2 Descriptive statistics of the partial correlation coefficients, *t*-test, and Shapiro–Wilk normality test of collected estimates

Study type	*K*	*Mean*	*Median*	*S.D.*	*Max.*	*Min.*	*Kurtosis*	*Skewness*	*t-test*[a]	*Shapiro-Wilk normality test (z)*[b]
All studies	759	0.135	0.163	0.313	0.896	−0.910	3.177	−0.227	11.910***	3.522†††
Studies of the whole of Asia	160	0.218	0.259	0.306	0.833	−0.456	2.594	−0.087	9.017***	2.916†††
Studies of East Asia	332	0.062	0.072	0.306	0.896	−0.910	3.213	−0.184	3.684***	1.677††
Studies of South Asia	267	0.177	0.201	0.307	0.893	−0.796	3.595	−0.404	9.430***	3.231†††

Notes

[a] *** Null hypothesis that the mean is zero is rejected at the 1% level

[b] ††† Null hypothesis of normal distribution is rejected at the 1% level; †† at the 5% level

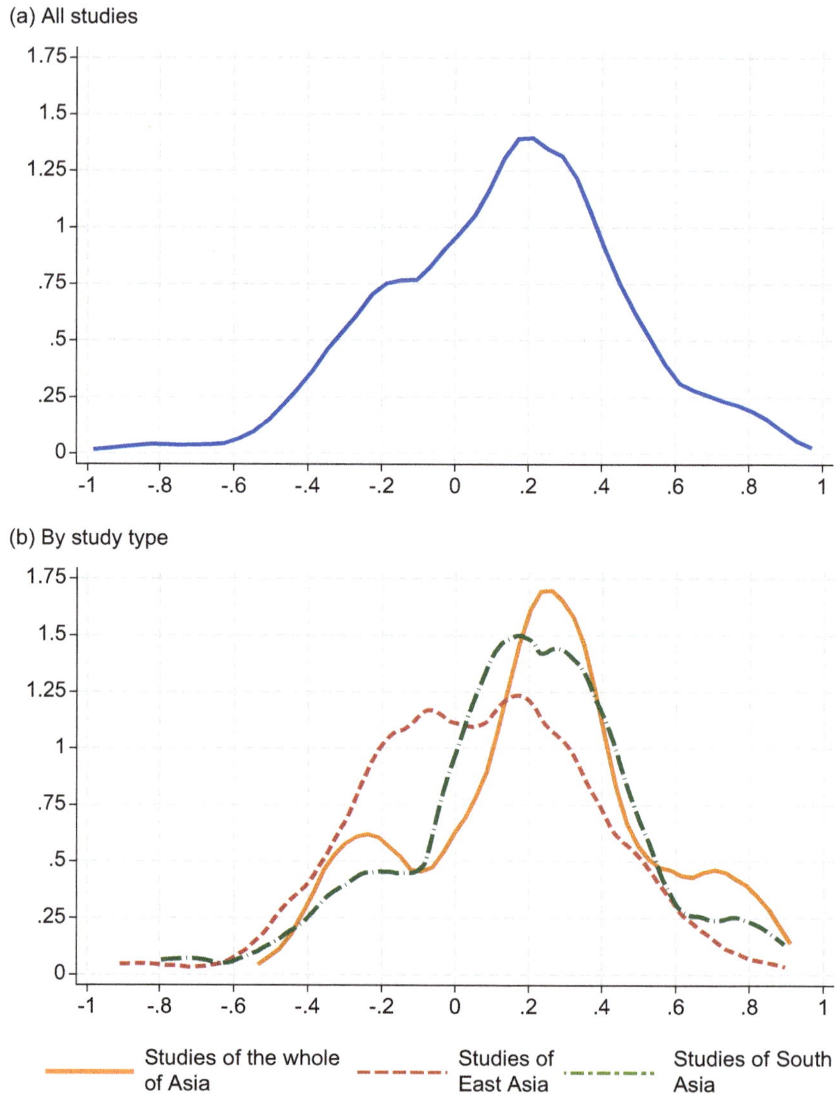

Fig. 3.2 Kernel density estimation of the collected estimates. *Notes* The vertical axis is the kernel density. The horizontal axis is the partial correlation coefficient of the collected estimates. See Table 3.2 for the descriptive statistics of the collected estimates

Table 3.3 Names, definitions, and descriptive statistics of meta-independent variables

Variable name	*Definition*	*Descriptive statistics*		
		Mean	*Median*	*S.D.*
Whole of Asia	1 = if target region is the whole of Asia, 0 = otherwise	0.211	0	0.408
East Asia	1 = if target region is East Asia, 0 = otherwise	0.437	0	0.496
South Asia	1 = if target region is South and Inner Asia, 0 = otherwise	0.352	0	0.478
Number of target countries	Total number of target countries	3.596	1	6.280
Share of developed countries	Share of developed countries in all target countries	0.131	0	0.293
Average year of estimation	Average year of estimation period	1995.245	1994.5	7.960
Length of estimation	Years of estimation period	25.946	23	11.651
Panel data	1 = if panel data is employed for empirical analysis, 0 = otherwise	0.644	1	0.479
Cross-sectional data	1 = if cross-sectional data is employed for empirical analysis, 0 = otherwise	0.016	0	0.125
Time-series data	1 = if time-series data is employed for empirical analysis, 0 = otherwise	0.340	0	0.474
Non-OLS	1 = if an estimator other than OLS is used for estimation, 0 = otherwise	0.706	1	0.456
OLS	1 = if an OLS estimator is used for estimation, 0 = otherwise	0.294	0	0.456
GDP per capita	1 = if the unit of the growth variable is real GDP per capita, 0 = otherwise	0.742	1	0.438
Real GDP	1 = if the unit of the growth variable is real GDP, 0 = otherwise	0.207	0	0.405
Nominal GDP	1 = if the unit of the growth variable is nominal GDP, 0 = otherwise	0.051	0	0.221

(continued)

Table 3.3 (continued)

Variable name	*Definition*	*Descriptive statistics*		
		Mean	*Median*	*S.D.*
Private credit to GDP	1 = if the financial variable is the ratio of private credit to GDP, 0 = otherwise	0.224	0	0.417
Financial depth	1 = if the financial variable captures the degree of financial depth, 0 = otherwise	0.111	0	0.314
Bank credit to GDP	1 = if the financial variable is the ratio of bank credit to GDP, 0 = otherwise	0.094	0	0.291
Private credit to domestic credit	1 = if the financial variable is the ratio of private credit to domestic credit, 0 = otherwise	0.009	0	0.096
Market capitalization	1 = if the financial variable captures the degree of market capitalization, 0 = otherwise	0.111	0	0.314
Stock market activity	1 = if the financial variable captures the degree of stock market activity, 0 = otherwise	0.088	0	0.284
Turnover ratio	1 = if the financial variable is the turnover ratio, 0 = otherwise	0.057	0	0.231
Comprehensive FD index	1 = if the financial variable is the comprehensive financial development index, 0 = otherwise	0.141	0	0.348
Other FD variables	1 = if a variable is used other than private credit to GDP and the above financial development variables, 0 = otherwise	0.040	0	0.195
Capital account openness	1 = if the financial variable captures the degree of capital account openness, 0 = otherwise	0.045	0	0.207
Financial market liberalization	1 = if the financial variable captures the degree of financial market liberalization, 0 = otherwise	0.030	0	0.172

(continued)

Table 3.3 (continued)

Variable name	*Definition*	*Descriptive statistics*		
		Mean	*Median*	*S.D.*
Stock market liberalization	1 = if the financial variable captures the degree of stock market liberalization, 0 = otherwise	0.040	0	0.195
Comprehensive FL index	1 = if the financial variable is the comprehensive financial liberalization index, 0 = otherwise	0.004	0	0.063
Other FL variables	1 = if a variable is used other than the above financial liberalization variables, 0 = otherwise	0.008	0	0.089
Lagged	1 = if the financial variable is lagged, 0 = otherwise	0.117	0	0.322
With intercepted variable	1 = if the financial variable is estimated with an intercepted variable(s), 0 = otherwise	0.103	0	0.304
Macroeconomic stability	1 = if estimation simultaneously controls for macroeconomic stability, 0 = otherwise	0.212	0	0.409
Trade openness	1 = if estimation simultaneously controls for trade openness, 0 = otherwise	0.497	0	0.500
Investment	1 = if estimation simultaneously controls for investment including capital formation, 0 = otherwise	0.406	0	0.491
Financial crisis	1 = if estimation simultaneously controls for financial crisis, 0 = otherwise	0.173	0	0.378
SE	Standard error of the partial correlation coefficient	0.103	0.086	0.053

Note The variables of the whole of Asia, panel data, non-OLS, GDP per capita, and private credit to GDP are used as default categories

Table 3.3, introduced in the previous section, complements this picture by detailing the coding frequencies and definitions of the moderator variables. Together, these descriptive analyses highlight a literature that is both rich and fragmented—a body of evidence whose complexity demands careful multivariate modeling to uncover systematic patterns.

In sum, the combination of Tables 3.2, 3.3 and Fig. 3.2 offers a multidimensional portrait of the evidence base, setting the stage for the meta-regression analyses that follow.

3.7 Transparency and Replication Materials

This study follows current best practices in meta-analytic research by emphasizing transparency, reproducibility, and open access to all analytical materials. Given that the credibility of a meta-analysis rests on the integrity of its data extraction, transformation, and estimation procedures, each stage of this process has been carefully documented and made available to the scholarly community.

All replication materials—including the dataset of extracted estimates, coding protocols, Stata do-files, and documentation of moderator variable definitions—are archived in a dedicated online repository hosted on Appendices A and B. The repository includes:

- A full bibliographic list of the 79 studies included in the meta-analysis;
- The dataset of 759 PCCs, with accompanying t-statistics, degrees of freedom, and standard errors;
- Variable codebook detailing the construction, coding logic, and frequency of all moderators used in the meta-regression analysis;
- Scripts for all major analyses, including descriptive statistics, synthesis estimations, Bayesian Model Averaging (BMA), Weighted-Average Least Squares (WALS), and publication bias diagnostics;
- Graphical outputs such as kernel density plots, funnel plots, and BMA inclusion maps.

In line with the guidelines proposed by Stanley and Doucouliagos (2012) and Havranek and Sokolova (2020), the transformation of raw estimates into PCCs is fully replicable, with each estimate linked to its source study and its original regression specification. The repository also includes a summary log of decision rules applied during the screening and coding process, including justifications for exclusion (e.g., insufficient statistical information or duplication between working papers and final publications).

To minimize error and bias, all coding was cross-verified by the authors, and a subset of estimates was independently reviewed for validation. Discrepancies were resolved through direct consultation of the original studies. Studies for which necessary test statistics could not be retrieved were excluded from quantitative analysis and are listed separately for reference. The repository will remain open for public use and academic engagement. Users are encouraged to cite the replication materials when reusing or extending the dataset. Suggestions for refinement or expansion are welcome, and any substantive revisions will be version-controlled to ensure future traceability.

By providing full replication materials, this project aims to contribute not only to the empirical understanding of the finance–growth–globalization nexus in Asia, but also to the broader meta-analytic community seeking to enhance transparency and cumulative knowledge in economic research.

Notes

1. The following academic press websites are used in this literature search: Emerald Insight, Oxford University Press, Sage Journals, Science Direct, Springer Link, Taylor and Francis Online, and Wiley Online Library. The search of academic press websites is conducted for the most recent studies, published since January 2021, to supplement the results of the EconLit search. The final literature search was conducted in July 2024.
2. Bibliography of 79 papers selected for meta-analysis is available upon request.
3. Table A1 provides the list of studies included for the meta-study, and Appendix B provides complete references of the 79 studies from which these effect sizes were extracted.

CHAPTER 4

Methodological Framework—Meta-Regression Techniques and Innovations

4.1 Why Meta-Analysis? Strengths and Limitations

Meta-analysis has emerged as a powerful tool in empirical economics for synthesizing findings across diverse studies. In research areas characterized by methodological fragmentation and contextual variability—such as the finance–growth–globalization nexus in Asia—meta-analysis offers a systematic way to assess the prevailing patterns and implications emerging from the broader body of evidence. Rather than privileging a single study or approach, meta-analysis draws on the collective insights of the literature, allowing for more generalizable inferences and a deeper understanding of conditional patterns.

The strengths of meta-analysis rest on both its statistical rigor and its ability to impose analytical structure on complexity. First, meta-analysis enables researchers to convert heterogeneous empirical results into a common metric—such as the partial correlation coefficient (PCC-explained below)—which allows for meaningful aggregation and comparison. As noted in Chap. 3, this standardization is essential given the diversity of functional forms, estimation techniques, and data structures used across the literature on financial development in Asia. Without such a transformation, differences in reported coefficients would remain incomparable, limiting the potential for coherent synthesis.

A. Anwar, I. Iwasaki, *Meta-Analysis of Finance and Growth in Asia*,
https://doi.org/10.1007/978-3-032-10219-5_4

Second, meta-analysis facilitates the detection and modeling of systematic heterogeneity. It is well understood that the effects of financial development or globalization on economic growth are not uniform. Differences in institutional quality, financial structure, regulatory regimes, and macroeconomic conditions can all mediate the observed relationship. Meta-regression techniques allow these sources of variation to be formally tested by regressing the standardized effect sizes on study-specific or country-level moderators. In doing so, meta-analysis shifts the focus from identifying a "true" average effect to uncovering conditional patterns and contextual dependencies—a key objective of this volume.

Third, meta-analysis allows researchers to address publication selection bias and related distortions that affect the interpretation of empirical results. As demonstrated in numerous fields, statistically significant or theoretically consistent findings are more likely to be published, a process that can skew the perceived consensus in the literature. Meta-analytic methods include a suite of tools to detect and adjust for such biases, enhancing the credibility and robustness of conclusions (Stanley & Doucouliagos, 2012; Ioannidis et al., 2017).

Yet, meta-analysis is not without limitations. Its quality depends fundamentally on the transparency and precision of the primary studies. Poorly reported or inconsistently estimated results weaken the empirical foundation of the meta-analytic exercise. This is particularly relevant in developing-country contexts, where data constraints or reporting omissions are more frequent. Moreover, the unit of analysis in meta-analysis is the estimate, not the study, which raises issues of interdependence. Multiple estimates from a single study may not be statistically independent, especially if derived from the same sample or closely related models. While modern meta-regression frameworks account for this via clustering, robust standard errors, or hierarchical modeling, it remains a challenge to avoid over-weighting studies with large numbers of estimates.

Finally, the interpretation of results requires caution. A statistically significant meta-average may reflect central tendencies in the literature, but it should not be interpreted as evidence of a universally applicable relationship. Likewise, meta-regression coefficients explain variation in published estimates, not direct causal relationships in the real world. As such, the contribution of meta-analysis is best understood as diagnostic and inferential: it identifies patterns, detects regularities, and reveals where additional research is most needed.

In sum, the rationale for adopting meta-analysis in this study is clear. It enables the systematic integration of a diverse literature, provides tools to explore heterogeneity and bias, and generates empirical insights that would be difficult to derive from narrative synthesis or conventional econometric replication alone. While it has limitations, meta-analysis offers a uniquely powerful framework for mapping and interpreting the evolving evidence base on financial development and globalization in Asia.

4.2 Meta-Analytic Estimation Strategy: Synthesis, Heterogeneity, and Model Uncertainty

This section outlines the first stage of our meta-analytic framework—statistical synthesis—by which we aggregate the collected effect sizes into a coherent summary. This synthesis serves as a foundation for modeling heterogeneity and evaluating robustness in subsequent stages.[1] According to Stanley and Doucouliagos (2012) and Iwasaki (2020ab), a meta-analysis conventionally consists of three steps: (a) meta-synthesis of collected estimates, (b) meta-regression analysis (MRA) of heterogeneity across studies, and (c) testing for publication selection bias. We follow this standard procedure.

To synthesize and compare estimates extracted from studies subject to meta-analysis, we employ the PCC. The PCC is a measure of the association of a dependent variable and the independent variable in question when other variables are held constant. The PCC is calculated in the following equation:

$$r_k = \frac{t_k}{\sqrt{t_k^2 + df_k}}, \ k = 1,\ 2,\ \ldots,\ K, \tag{4.1}$$

where t_k and df_k denote the t value and the degree of freedom of the k–th estimate, respectively, while K denotes the total number of collected estimates.[2] The standard error (SE) of r_k is given by $\sqrt{(1 - r_k^2)/df_k}$.[3]

To synthesize the collected estimates, we utilize the unrestricted weighted least squares average (UWA), and the weighted average of the adequately powered (WAAP) in addition to the conventional meta-fixed-effect and random-effects methods. While the fixed-effect and random-effects models have long been used in conventional meta-analyses, recent research has shown that the UWA and WAAP methods offer improved performance in the presence of high heterogeneity and selective reporting (Stanley et al., 2017). Accordingly, we prioritize WAAP as the primary synthesis estimator in this study. The UWA is used as a complementary estimator, while the fixed—and random-effects models serve as benchmark references for comparison purposes.

According to Stanley and Doucouliagos (2017) and Stanley et al. (2017), the UWA is less subject to influence from excess heterogeneity than is the meta-fixed-effect model. The UWA method regards the synthesized effect size as a point estimate obtained from the regression that takes the standardized effect size as the dependent variable and the estimation precision as the independent variable. Specifically, we estimate Eq. (4.1), in which there is no intercept term, and the coefficient, α, is utilized as the synthesized value of the collected estimates in question:

$$t_k = \alpha(1/SE_k) + \varepsilon_k, \tag{4.2}$$

where SE_k is the standard error of the k–th estimate, and ε_k is a residual term. In theory, α in Eq. (4.2) is consistent with the estimate of the meta-fixed-effect model.

Further, Stanley et al. (2017) proposed conducting a UWA of estimates, the statistical power of which exceeds the threshold of 0.80, and called this estimation method "the weighted average of the adequately powered (WAAP)." They stated that WAAP synthesis has less publication selection bias than the traditional meta-random-effects model. Accordingly, we adopt the WAAP estimate as the best synthesis value whenever available. Otherwise, the traditional synthesized effect size is used as the second-best reference value.

4.3 Bayesian and Frequentist Approaches (BMA, WALS)

A central challenge in MRA is the presence of model uncertainty—the empirical reality that multiple plausible models exist, each containing different combinations of explanatory variables, but no single model can be known ex ante to represent the true data-generating process. This issue is especially pronounced in research areas such as the finance–growth–globalization nexus, where the literature draws on varied empirical strategies, variable definitions, and regional contexts. As Havranek and Sokolova (2020) and Zigraiova et al. (2021) emphasize, model uncertainty, if left unaddressed, can compromise the reliability and generalizability of regression-based inference in meta-analytic settings.

To mitigate this problem, we adopt two complementary variable selection techniques: Bayesian Model Averaging (BMA) and Weighted-Average Least Squares (WALS). Both approaches are specifically designed to handle model uncertainty and are widely used in recent empirical meta-analyses. This is particularly important in the present context, where the diversity of functional forms, country samples, and econometric strategies across the literature complicates variable selection using traditional step-wise or theory-driven methods.

The BMA framework operates from a Bayesian perspective. It evaluates the posterior inclusion probability (PIP) for each moderator, based on how frequently and significantly that variable appears across the best-fitting models. The PIP can be interpreted as the likelihood that a given variable belongs to the true model, conditional on the data and the prior model space. A threshold of PIP ≥0.50 is commonly used in the literature to identify variables with meaningful explanatory weight. This approach allows for systematic evaluation of all possible model permutations and accommodates correlation among moderators.

In contrast, WALS belongs to the frequentist tradition. It combines weighted least squares (WLS) estimation with shrinkage techniques to produce stable coefficient estimates, even in the presence of multicollinearity or overparameterization. Unlike traditional model selection methods, which commit to a single model, WALS averages over a large class of models, applying data-driven weights to reflect the relative informativeness of each variable. A t-statistic threshold of 1.00 or greater is used to retain moderators with moderate and stable predictive strength. This approach avoids over-fitting and enhances robustness to outliers and sampling variation.

While the two methods are grounded in different statistical philosophies, their combined use offers a more robust and cross-validated path to identifying empirically relevant moderators. BMA provides probabilistic inclusion metrics, while WALS offers frequentist consistency checks. When used together, these methods allow us to narrow the list of potential moderators in a way that is both methodologically conservative and empirically grounded. This dual-filter strategy ensures that retained moderators exhibit explanatory strength across distinct statistical paradigms, thereby enhancing the internal validity and interpretive reliability of the subsequent MRA.

In applying BMA and WALS to our dataset, we aim not to identify a single "correct" model, but to establish a well-supported subset of variables that capture the most consistent patterns of heterogeneity across the empirical literature. These selected moderators then form the basis for the full estimation strategy outlined in the next section.

4.4 Meta-Regression Models and Robustness Strategy

Following the identification of relevant moderators through BMA and WALS, we proceed to the core stage of our analysis: estimating a series of meta-regression models that quantify the heterogeneity in reported effect sizes across studies. This step enables us to assess how study-level characteristics—such as estimation techniques, variable definitions, and regional contexts—systematically influence the finance–growth–globalization relationship observed in the empirical literature.

As shown in Eq. (4.3), the underlying meta-regression framework takes the following form:

$$y_k = \beta_0 + \sum_{n=1}^{N} \beta_n x_{kn} + \beta_{SE} SE_k + e_k, \tag{4.3}$$

where y_k is the k–th estimate, β_0 is the constant, x_{kn} denotes a meta-independent variable (also known as a moderator) that captures the relevant characteristics of an empirical study and explains its systematic variation from other empirical results in the literature, β_n denotes the meta-regression coefficient to be estimated. β_{SE} expresses the coefficient of SE, and e_k is the meta-regression disturbance term. Each meta-regression includes two regional indicators (East Asia and South Asia, with studies on Asia as a whole as the reference group) and the subset of moderators identified through the BMA/WALS selection procedure outlined in Sect. 4.3.

While the functional form is conventional in meta-analysis, there is no clear consensus in the literature regarding the optimal estimation approach (Iwasaki et al., 2020; Ono & Iwasaki, 2022). Given the high likelihood of heteroskedasticity, within-study dependence, and structural clustering, we employ a multiestimator strategy to ensure that findings are not overly sensitive to any single model specification.

We begin by accounting for unobserved heterogeneity at the study level. In cases where unobserved effects may be correlated with the moderators, we estimate a fixed-effects panel least squares dummy variable (LSDV) model. When the assumption of orthogonality between moderators and unobserved study-level heterogeneity is plausible, we use a random-effects generalized least squares (GLS) estimator. The decision between these two estimators is guided by the Hausman specification test, which determines whether the GLS estimator yields consistent estimates relative to the LSDV benchmark. We initially consider both fixed-effects (LSDV) and random-effects (GLS) panel estimators. However, based on the Hausman specification test, we retain the random-effects GLS estimator, which assumes orthogonality between moderators and unobserved heterogeneity.

In addition to these panel estimators, we apply three cluster-robust WLS variants, each designed to address different dimensions of within-study dependence and sample heterogeneity:

- WLS weighted by the inverse of the standard error ($1/SE$), the traditional precision-weighted approach widely used in meta-analysis;
- WLS weighted by degrees of freedom, to adjust for differences in sample sizes across studies and enhance comparability;
- WLS weighted by the inverse number of estimates per study to prevent studies contributing many estimates from disproportionately influencing the overall results.

We also employ a multilevel mixed-effects robust linear model (RLM) that explicitly models the nested structure of meta-analytic data, allowing for random intercepts at the study level. This estimator is particularly well-suited for datasets that combine multiple observations from individual studies, as it allows for partial pooling and reduces the risk of downward-biased standard errors. These estimation strategies correspond to the five model columns in Table 5.3, labeled by their analytical weights: inverse standard error [$1/SE$], degrees of freedom [*df*], inverse number of estimates per study [$1/EST$], multilevel mixed-effects (RLM), and random-effects panel GLS.

To assess the robustness of moderator effects across these five distinct estimators, we apply a triangulation rule adapted from Iwasaki et al. (2020): a moderator is considered robust if it is statistically significant and maintains the same sign in at least three out of the five estimation techniques. This approach balances statistical rigor with empirical flexibility, ensuring that retained effects are not artifacts of specific modeling assumptions.

By deploying this battery of estimation techniques—ranging from panel regressions to multilevel and WLS models—we seek to maximize both internal validity and cross-method reliability. This strategy reflects the empirical complexity of a literature that is not only theoretically diverse but also methodologically heterogeneous. Ultimately, the aim is to isolate the most consistent, interpretable, and policy-relevant patterns of variation in how globalization and financial development interact to shape economic growth outcomes in Asia.

4.5 Examination of Publication Selection Bias (Funnel Tests, FAT, PET, and PEESE)

A recurring concern in meta-analysis—especially within literatures characterized by policy relevance and strong theoretical priors—is the risk of publication selection bias. This bias arises when the probability of a study entering the published record is not random but systematically related to the nature or statistical significance of its findings. In the context of the finance–growth–globalization literature, this tendency can manifest as a preference for "positive" or confirmatory results—those that report statistically significant associations, conform to conventional expectations, or lend support to dominant policy narratives.

As Stanley and Doucouliagos (2012) and Cazachevici et al. (2020) emphasize, such biases may not be conscious or deliberate. Rather, they are often the result of structural incentives within academic publishing and research funding, which collectively favor results that are novel, statistically significant, and directionally interpretable. When this occurs, the available literature becomes skewed—overrepresenting significant effects and underreporting null, negative, or ambiguous results. Consequently, the empirical landscape that meta-analysis seeks to summarize may already be filtered, and any synthesis based on such a sample risks overestimating the true underlying effect.

To explore this possibility, we begin with the funnel plot, a standard visual diagnostic tool in meta-analytic practice. A funnel plot charts the distribution of effect sizes (in our case, PPCs) on the horizontal axis and their precision (defined as the inverse of the standard error) on the vertical axis. In the absence of selection bias, one would expect the plot to resemble a symmetric inverted funnel. Smaller studies (with larger standard errors) naturally produce more dispersed estimates due to sampling variability, while larger, more precise studies cluster near the population mean.

Symmetry around this central effect is taken as evidence that the dataset reflects a balanced cross-section of empirical findings.

However, when the funnel plot appears asymmetric—for instance, if negative or statistically insignificant estimates from small-sample studies are underrepresented—this suggests selective reporting. Such asymmetry signals that the literature may have been shaped by an implicit filter that elevates certain types of results while suppressing others. While this visual pattern is intuitive, it is also inherently subjective. Perceptions of symmetry may vary across observers, and deviations from the ideal funnel shape may result from legitimate heterogeneity, such as regional variation, estimation techniques, or sample composition.

To address these limitations, we employ the FAT–PET–PEESE procedure, developed by Stanley and Doucouliagos (2012), which provides formal statistical tests to detect and correct for publication selection bias. The first step is the funnel asymmetry test (FAT), which regresses the t-statistic of each estimate on the inverse of its standard error:

$$t_k = \gamma_0 + \gamma_1(1/SE_k) + v_k, \tag{4.4}$$

where v_k is the error term. When the intercept term γ_0 is statistically different from zero, we interpret this as evidence of publication selection bias affecting the dataset. This result does not, however, rule out the possibility that a genuine empirical effect exists.

To examine whether a real underlying relationship persists, we apply the precision effect test (PET), which uses the same regression framework but focuses on the slope coefficient γ_1. If γ_1 is statistically significant, this indicates that more precise estimates tend to be associated with larger effect sizes. In such cases, even if selection bias is present, the literature may still contain a true signal, albeit one distorted in magnitude.

To estimate that signal, we implement the precision effect estimate with standard error (PEESE) model. This version modifies the regression by including the standard error as an additional regressor and omitting the intercept:

$$t_k = \varphi_0 SE_k + \varphi_1(1/SE_k) + w_k, \tag{4.5}$$

where w_k is the error term. This is the PEESE approach. If φ_1 is statistically significant, it provides a corrected estimate of the underlying effect size—adjusted for bias arising from nonrandom publication.

To test the robustness of the coefficients obtained from the above FAT–PET–PEESE procedure, we estimate Eqs. (4.4) and (4.5) using not only the unrestricted WLS estimator, but also the WLS estimator with bootstrapped standard errors, the cluster-robust WLS estimator, and the unbalanced panel estimator for a robustness check. In addition to these four models, we also run an instrumental variable (IV) estimation with the inverse of the square root of the number of observations used as an instrument of the standard error, because "the standard error can be endogenous if some method choices affect both the estimate and the standard error. Moreover, the standard error is estimated, which causes attenuation bias in meta-analysis" (Cazachevici et al., 2020, p. 5).

4.6 Robustness Checks and Alternative Approaches to Bias Correction

In addition to the FAT–PET–PEESE framework, we apply a set of alternative techniques that have been developed in recent years to estimate publication selection bias–adjusted effect sizes. These methods serve as robustness checks and offer useful comparisons to the PEESE estimates used in the main analysis.

One such method is the Top 10 approach, introduced by Stanley et al. (2010), which proposes discarding 90% of the available estimates and synthesizing only the most precise 10%. This strategy dramatically reduces the influence of publication selection by concentrating on high-powered estimates and has been shown to outperform conventional summary statistics under certain conditions.

A second approach is the selection model developed by Andrews and Kasy (2019), which estimates the conditional probability of publication based on a study's results. This model explicitly accounts for the idea that the probability of an estimate appearing in the literature may depend on its statistical significance or direction, and corrects accordingly.

The third method is the endogenous kinked model, proposed by Bom and Rachinger (2019). This technique models the relationship between effect sizes and their standard errors using a piecewise linear regression with a "kink" at a threshold standard error. Estimates below this kink are assumed to be less subject to selection, allowing for a bias-corrected extrapolation of the true effect.

Finally, we apply the p-uniform method, introduced by van Aert and van Assen (2012). This approach is based on the statistical theory that, conditional on a true population effect, the distribution of significant p-values should be uniform. Departures from uniformity signal the presence of publication bias, which the method adjusts for to recover the underlying effect size.

Each of these techniques is applied to the dataset to generate alternative estimates of the publication bias–adjusted effect size. We then compare these results with those obtained from the PEESE method to assess consistency and evaluate the sensitivity of our conclusions to different correction frameworks. Together, these robustness checks strengthen the credibility of the findings and demonstrate that the core results are not an artifact of any one estimation strategy.

Last, the literature selection and meta-analysis in this book comply with the reporting guidelines for meta-analysis in economics described in Havránek et al. (2020).

4.7 Summary of Analytical Strategy

This chapter has outlined the analytical framework used to synthesize and examine the large and diverse body of empirical research on the finance–growth–globalization nexus in Asia. The goal of this section is to summarize that framework in accessible terms, highlighting key steps and safeguards in clear, nontechnical terms.

The analysis begins with a comprehensive dataset of effect size estimates drawn from 79 studies. These estimates capture the reported relationship between financial development and economic growth across different Asian countries and time periods. Because the original studies vary widely in their methods, variables, and model forms, we first standardize the results into a common metric—known as the PCC—so they can be meaningfully compared.

The core of the analysis is a meta-regression, a statistical method that helps us understand why some studies report stronger or weaker results than others. Instead of assuming all studies are estimating the same effect, we treat the variation in results as meaningful and aim to explain it. This is done by identifying patterns in how study characteristics—such as country focus, time period, estimation technique, or type of financial indicator used—relate to the reported outcomes.

To ensure that our conclusions are not overly sensitive to a particular statistical model, we use multiple estimation approaches. These include several variants of weighted regression and panel-based techniques that adjust for differences in study quality and dependence among estimates. We treat a result as robust only if it appears consistently across several models, reflecting a conservative approach to inference.

We also take explicit steps to detect and correct for publication selection bias, the tendency for studies with statistically significant or theoretically expected results to be more likely published. This is done using both visual diagnostics (funnel plots) and a set of formal statistical tools (FAT–PET–PEESE). Additionally, we apply newer correction methods—such as the Top 10 estimator and selection models—to verify that our findings are not artifacts of selective reporting.

Together, this multistage strategy allows us to account for methodological diversity, ensure comparability across studies, and isolate the most reliable empirical patterns. The aim is not to force consensus, but to understand variation—highlighting where, when, and why finance and globalization appear to shape growth outcomes across Asia.

Notes

1. The methodological description of the meta-analysis presented in this section is concise due to space constraints. For further details, refer to Stanley and Doucouliagos (2012) and Borenstein et al. (2021). A practitioner's guide to meta-analysis of social science research by Irsova et al. (2024) also provides valuable insights into the fundamentals of meta-analysis.
2. A benefit of the PCC is that it makes comparing and synthesizing collected estimates easier concerning independent variables of which the definitions or units differ. On the other hand, a flaw of the PCC is that its distribution is not normal when the coefficient is close to -1 or $+1$ (Stanley & Doucouliagos, 2012). Fisher's z-transformation is the most well-known solution to this problem. As in overall economic studies, the PCC of each estimate used for our meta-analysis is rarely observed to be close to the upper or lower limit; thus, we use the PCC as calculated in Eq. (4.1) throughout the book.
3. We use this formula to compute the standard error of partial correlation coefficient, following the example of Stanley and Doucouliagos (2023), who point out that the other formula $\left(1 - r_k^2/\sqrt{df_k}\right)$ that better reflects the variation of the sampling distribution of PCCs is not appropriate for meta-analysis because its PCC variance tends to cause random effects to be more biased than the formula we adopt.

CHAPTER 5

Empirical Findings from the Meta-Analysis

This chapter presents the core empirical results of the meta-analysis, beginning with meta-synthesis, followed by meta-regression analysis (MRA), robustness checks, and bias correction procedures. Before turning to the main findings, it is useful to briefly recall the structure of the dataset underpinning these analyses. As summarized in Sect. 3.6, the sample comprises 759 partial correlation coefficients (PCCs) extracted from 79 studies, encompassing a wide range of countries, time periods, and methodological approaches. The distribution of these estimates is broadly centered on a modestly positive mean, but with considerable heterogeneity—particularly across regions. These descriptive features provide the empirical backdrop against which the following analytical results should be interpreted.

5.1 Meta-Synthesis of Collected Estimates

We begin our empirical investigation with a meta-synthesis of the 759 collected effect sizes (PCCs), estimating average effects of financial development and liberalization on economic growth across all studies and by region. Table 5.1 summarizes the results of both traditional and newly proposed synthesis techniques.

The synthesis is conducted in three stages. First, we report conventional fixed-effect and random-effects meta-estimates (Column a). Second, we

A. Anwar, I. Iwasaki, *Meta-Analysis of Finance and Growth in Asia*,
https://doi.org/10.1007/978-3-032-10219-5_5

Table 5.1 Synthesis of collected estimates

Study type	*Number of estimates (K)*	*(a) Traditional synthesis*		*(b) Heterogeneity test and measures*			*(c) Unrestricted weighted least squares average (UWA)*				
		Fixed-effect model (z value)[a]	*Random-effects model (z value)*[a]	*Cochran Q test of homogeneity (p value)*[b]	*I^2 statistic*[c]	*H^2 statistic*[d]	*UWA of all estimates (t value)*[a, e]	*Number of adequately powered estimates*[f]	*WAAP (weighted average of adequately powered estimates) (t value)*[a]	*Median S. E. of estimates*	*Median statistical power*
All studies	759	0.065 *** (26.84)	0.133 *** (11.75)	13,734.10 *** (0.00)	95.05	20.18	0.065 *** (6.31)	22	**0.095** *** **(9.17)**	0.086	0.113
Studies of the whole of Asia	160	0.233 *** (43.32)	0.220 *** (9.08)	3145.34 *** (0.00)	95.00	95.00	0.233 *** (9.74)	70	**0.294** *** **(7.91)**	0.085	0.780
Studies of East Asia	332	−0.005 * (−1.81)	**0.057** *** **(3.55)**	6841.18 *** (0.00)	96.22	26.43	−0.005 (−0.40)	0	- (-)	0.077	0.029
Studies of South Asia	267	0.145 *** (23.01)	0.174 *** (9.14)	2058.88 *** (0.00)	88.25	8.51	0.145 *** (8.27)	4	**0.103** *** **(10.50)**	0.132	0.193

Notes *** and * denote statistical significance at the 1% and 10% levels, respectively. Selected synthesis values are emphasized in bold [a] Null hypothesis: The synthesized effect size is zero [b] Null hypothesis: Effect sizes are homogeneous [c] Ranges between 0 and 100% with larger scores indicating heterogeneity [d] Takes zero in the case of homogeneity [e] Synthesis method advocated by Stanley and Doucouliagos (2017) and Stanley et al. (2017) [f] Denotes the number of estimates with a statistical power of 0.80 or more that is computed in reference to the UWA of all collected estimates assess heterogeneity in effect sizes using the Cochran Q test, I^2 and H^2 statistics (Column b). Finally, we apply the unrestricted weighted least squares average (UWA) and the weighted average of adequately powered estimates (WAAP) as proposed by Stanley and Doucouliagos (2017), with results shown in Column (c).

In the traditional synthesis, the fixed-effect model assumes a common true effect across all studies, while the random-effects model allows for variation in true effect sizes due to between-study heterogeneity. As shown in Column (a), the fixed-effect estimate for all studies is 0.065, while the random-effects estimate rises to 0.133. For studies of the whole of Asia and South Asia, the synthesized effects are larger (0.233 and 0.145, respectively), while for East Asia, the random-effects estimate is just 0.057—barely distinguishable from zero.

To determine whether these variations are statistically meaningful, we perform heterogeneity tests. Column (b) shows that the Cochran Q test strongly rejects the null of homogeneity in all four groups ($p < 0.01$), and the I^2 statistics exceed 88% in every case, indicating substantial heterogeneity. This justifies the preference for the random-effects model over the fixed-effect model as a baseline reference. Yet, even the random-effects model can be sensitive to outliers and model specification. To address this, we adopt the UWA, estimated using Eq. (5.1):

$$t_k = \alpha(1/SE_k) + \epsilon_k \tag{5.1}$$

In this formulation, the t value t_k is regressed on its precision ($1/SE_k$), without an intercept, yielding a synthesized effect (α) that is less biased by excess heterogeneity. Column (c) of Table 5.1 reports these UWA estimates. For all studies, the UWA estimate (0.065) matches the fixed-effect value, but its t_k-value is smaller—indicating that UWA is more conservative under heterogeneity. More importantly, UWA is also the basis for computing the WAAP, which includes only estimates with statistical power ≥0.80.

The WAAP results are particularly noteworthy. For three of the four categories—All Studies, Whole of Asia, and South Asia—WAAP estimates are successfully computed and statistically significant. Specifically, the WAAP value is 0.095 for all studies, 0.294 for studies of the whole of Asia, and 0.103 for South Asia. These figures represent our preferred estimates, as they reflect more credible synthesis under high heterogeneity and mitigate the effects of publication selection bias (Stanley et al., 2017). For East Asia, however, no estimates met the 0.80 power threshold, so the random-effects estimate of 0.057 is retained as the reference value.

To interpret the economic meaning of these estimates, we follow Doucouliagos (2011), who classifies PCCs of 0.10–0.20 as "small" and those above 0.25 as "moderate".[1] Against this benchmark:

- The WAAP estimate of 0.095 for all studies suggests a **small but statistically significant** average effect of financial development and liberalization on growth across Asia.
- The WAAP value of 0.294 for studies of the whole of Asia indicates a **moderate-sized effect,** reinforcing **Hypothesis** 1, which expects finance to support growth across Asian economies.
- The weak effect in East Asia (0.057, random-effects) compared to South Asia's 0.103 (WAAP) supports Hypothesis 2, which posits stronger marginal gains from financial development in South Asia, where baseline financial access is lower and leapfrogging effects are more plausible.

In sum, the synthesis results confirm a statistically significant and economically meaningful finance–growth link in Asia overall, with subregional variation. These findings lend strong support to Hypotheses 1 and 2. However, the synthesis methods used here do not account for potential differences in research design, sample periods, or econometric strategies across studies. For that reason, the Sect. 5.2 turns to multivariate MRA, which allows us to explain observed heterogeneity and test the robustness of these findings in a controlled setting.

5.2 Meta-Regression Analysis: Sources of Heterogeneity

This section investigates the sources of heterogeneity in the finance–growth relationship across Asia by leveraging two complementary estimation techniques: Bayesian Model Averaging (BMA) and Weighted-Average Least Squares (WALS). These methods address key econometric concerns in MRA, particularly model uncertainty and multicollinearity, which arise when numerous potential moderators are considered simultaneously.

As emphasized by Polák (2019) and Havranek and Sokolova (2020), model uncertainty reflects the empirical reality that no single "true" model can be known ex ante. Multiple combinations of moderators may plausibly explain variation in effect sizes, and selecting one arbitrarily risks specification bias. Furthermore, including several correlated moderators increases the risk of multicollinearity, distorting coefficient estimates and inference. Recent meta-analyses in economics have responded to these challenges by employing BMA and WALS as systematic variable selection and inference frameworks (e.g., Bajzik et al., 2020; Zigraiova et al., 2021; Anwar & Mang, 2022; Horie et al., 2024).

In this study, we apply BMA using the dilution prior advocated by George (2010), which penalizes model complexity and guards against overfitting when many variables are weakly informative. BMA assigns weights to each model based on its posterior model probability (PMP), which reflects how well the model fits the data relative to its complexity. Posterior inclusion probabilities (PIPs) are then computed for each meta-independent variable, indicating the likelihood that a given moderator belongs to the "true" model space.

To complement BMA, we also estimate a WALS model, which offers a frequentist alternative that linearly combines weighted least squares estimators across a large number of submodels (Magnus et al., 2010; De Luca & Magnus, 2011). Compared to BMA, WALS is computationally simpler, based on a transparent definition of prior ignorance, and often preferred in meta-regression settings involving collinearity (Ugur et al., 2020; Anwar & Mang, 2022). Unlike BMA's probabilistic interpretation, WALS selects variables based on the statistical significance of their coefficients, typically applying a threshold of $t \geq 1.96$.

In line with established practice, we adopt a dual selection rule: moderators are retained for inclusion in the final meta-regression model if they meet either of two criteria—PIP ≥0.50 in the BMA model or $t \geq 1.96$ in the WALS model. Table 5.2 presents the results from both estimators, including posterior means and standard deviations (BMA), and coefficients and t-values (WALS). Figure 5.1 provides a visual summary of model inclusion across the BMA process, highlighting the stability and prominence of selected moderators.

The results identify seven consistently robust moderators, ordered by strength of inclusion: market capitalization, capital account openness, stock market liberalization, financial market liberalization, turnover ratio, financial crisis, and average year of estimation. These variables appear in the

Table 5.2 Meta-regression analysis for the selection of moderators

Estimator	*Bayesian model averaging (BMA)*			*Weighted-average least squares (WALS)*		
Meta-independent variables/Model	*[1]*			*[2]*		
	Post mean	*Post S.D.*	*PIP*	*Coef.*	*S.E.*	*t*
Key regressors						
East Asia	−0.2230	0.0594	1.000	−0.2822	0.0588	−4.80
South Asia	−0.1444	0.0610	1.000	−0.1953	0.0609	−3.21
SE	0.2545	0.3046	1.000	0.0143	0.3055	0.05
Moderators to be selected						
Number of target countries	−0.0002	0.0010	0.043	−0.0006	0.0025	−0.26
Share of developed countries	−0.0002	0.0048	0.007	−0.0215	0.0476	−0.45
Average year of estimation	−0.0061	0.0030	0.858	−0.0062	0.0022	−2.79
Length of estimation	0.0000	0.0001	0.004	−0.0034	0.0019	−1.80
Cross-sectional data	0.0002	0.0065	0.004	0.0465	0.0834	0.56
Time-series data	0.0355	0.0695	0.235	0.1843	0.0515	3.57
OLS	0.0300	0.0365	0.452	0.0722	0.0215	3.36
Real GDP	0.0000	0.0028	0.007	−0.0590	0.0340	−1.73
Nominal GDP	−0.0093	0.0348	0.083	−0.0714	0.0607	−1.18
Financial depth	0.0182	0.0397	0.202	0.0569	0.0383	1.48
Bank credit to GDP	−0.0055	0.0227	0.069	−0.0693	0.0402	−1.72
Private credit to domestic credit	0.0000	0.0040	0.001	−0.0008	0.1053	−0.01
Market capitalization	0.2044	0.0368	1.000	0.1431	0.0399	3.59
Stock market activity	0.0081	0.0275	0.096	0.0409	0.0415	0.98
Turnover ratio	−0.1701	0.0841	0.867	−0.1734	0.0528	−3.29
Comprehensive FD index	−0.0004	0.0051	0.009	−0.0280	0.0375	−0.75
Other FD variables	−0.0315	0.0636	0.228	−0.1115	0.0549	−2.03
Capital account openness	−0.4038	0.0608	1.000	−0.3377	0.0540	−6.25

(continued)

Table 5.2 (continued)

Estimator	*Bayesian model averaging (BMA)*			*Weighted-average least squares (WALS)*		
Meta-independent variables/Model	*[1]*			*[2]*		
	Post mean	*Post S.D.*	*PIP*	*Coef.*	*S.E.*	*t*
Financial market liberalization	−0.3345	0.0746	0.998	−0.3016	0.0636	−4.74
Stock market liberalization	−0.3433	0.0656	1.000	−0.3046	0.0583	−5.23
Comprehensive FL index	−0.0011	0.0187	0.007	−0.0372	0.1464	−0.25
Other FL variables	0.0041	0.0323	0.024	0.1449	0.1067	1.36
Lagged	−0.0306	0.0561	0.264	−0.0958	0.0353	−2.71
With intercepted variable	0.0004	0.0052	0.010	0.0603	0.0333	1.81
Macroeconomic stability	0.0001	0.0026	0.007	0.0142	0.0264	0.54
Trade openness	0.0001	0.0029	0.007	0.0442	0.0279	1.58
Investment	0.0000	0.0014	0.003	0.0253	0.0239	1.06
Financial crisis	0.1569	0.0788	0.862	0.1376	0.0530	2.60
K	759			759		

Notes see Table 3.3 for the definitions and descriptive statistics of meta-independent variables. The estimate of the intercept is omitted. Coef., S.D., PIP, and S.E. denote coefficient, standard deviation, posterior inclusion probability, and standard errors, respectively

highest-ranked models in the BMA posterior distribution and are statistically significant in the WALS estimates. Collectively, they reflect key dimensions of both financial structure and historical context, providing a rich basis for explaining variation in the reported finance–growth effects.

The central insight from this analysis is that the finance–growth nexus in Asia remains positive on average, but its magnitude and significance depend heavily on financial structure and liberalization strategy. Our findings are consistent with previous global meta-analyses such as Arestis et al. (2015); Valickova et al. (2015); Brada and Iwasaki (2023); and Iwasaki and Kočenda (2024), all of which find that finance positively affects growth under certain institutional and market conditions.

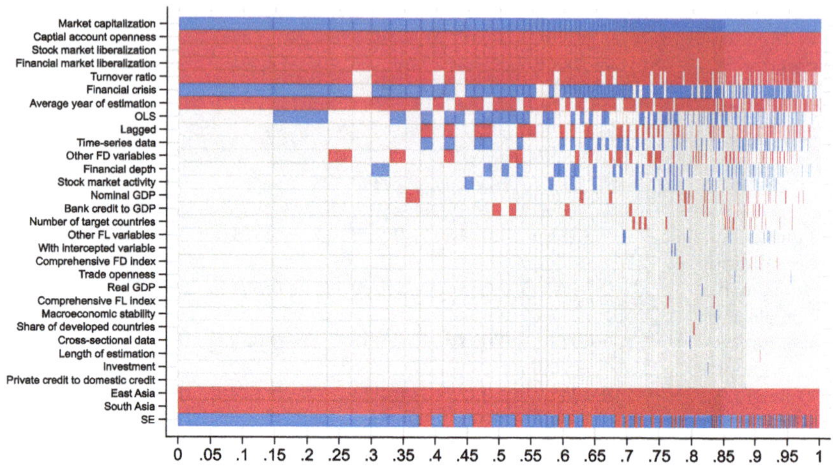

Fig. 5.1 Model inclusion in Bayesian model averaging (K = 759). *Notes* the response variable is the effect of financial development and liberalization on economic growth as measured by the partial correlation coefficient. Here, columns show regression models in individual studies; variables are sorted by PIPs in descending order. A blue (red) color depicts a positive (negative) impact of the explanatory variable on the response variable. No color means that the variable is not included in the model. The horizontal axis measures the cumulative PMP for the best 10,000 models. Estimates are weighted by the inverse variance. The vertical axis shows the list of explanatory variables, and the descriptions of these variables are presented in Table 3.3

Among the most influential moderators, market capitalization stands out. Both BMA and WALS identify this variable as having a large, positive, and statistically significant effect. This aligns with previous regional studies—such as Anwar and Iwasaki (2023a)—who report that stock market development, as proxied by capitalization, enhances growth in Middle Eastern and African economies. In Asia, Liu and Zhang (2020) also confirm that rising market capitalization stimulates banking sector expansion and broadens access to credit, thereby fueling investment and economic growth.

In contrast, our results challenge earlier expectations regarding the benefits of stock market liberalization and capital account openness. Although both variables have high PIPs and t-values, their estimated coefficients are negative—suggesting that, on average, liberalization efforts in these areas have not delivered the growth dividends often presumed. This finding echoes skepticism raised in recent literature about the efficacy of liberalization without sufficient regulatory infrastructure (Valickova et al., 2015; Estrada et al., 2015). One explanation is that stock market liberalization and capital mobility may introduce volatility and misallocation in financially underdeveloped systems, particularly where governance capacity is weak.

A similar story emerges for the turnover ratio, a proxy for market liquidity, which has a consistently negative coefficient. While higher liquidity is typically associated with efficiency, in the Asian context it may reflect speculative trading rather than productive capital allocation. This result lends support to Sharma and Kautish (2020), who argue that short-term shocks in Asia's capital markets often dominate long-term investment dynamics, undermining the growth potential of financial reforms.

The inclusion of financial crisis as a positive moderator may appear counterintuitive at first glance. However, it can be interpreted as capturing the post-crisis institutional reforms that often follow financial turbulence. For instance, several Asian economies undertook sweeping restructuring efforts after the 1997 Asian Financial Crisis and the 2008 global crisis, resulting in stronger banking supervision and macroprudential regulation—factors that may have supported subsequent growth.

Finally, average year of estimation appears as a negatively signed moderator, implying that reported finance–growth effects tend to decline in more recent studies. This trend may reflect greater data availability, better identification strategies, or growing publication of null results in the post-2008 research environment.

In sum, the BMA and WALS results underscore the importance of financial structure and historical context in shaping the finance–growth nexus in Asia. They also validate the need for flexible, data-driven estimation strategies that account for model uncertainty. These findings inform the full meta-regression analyses presented in the next section, where we estimate multivariate models using a battery of robustness checks and panel estimators to assess the stability and generalizability of these moderator effects.

5.3 Robust Analysis: Meta-Regression Analysis

As a robustness check, we estimate five versions of the meta-regression model using alternative estimators, following the triangulation strategy proposed by Iwasaki et al. (2020, 2022). These techniques are designed to address potential biases arising from heteroskedasticity, clustering, or sample-size imbalances in the dataset. Specifically, we apply the following:[2]

a. Cluster-robust WLS weighted by $1/SE$—the conventional precision-weighted estimator that clusters errors by study;
b. Cluster-robust WLS weighted by degrees of freedom (*d.f.*)—to adjust for cross-study variation in sample sizes;
c. Cluster-robust WLS weighted by the inverse number of estimates per study ($1/EST$)—to prevent overweighting prolific studies;
d. Multilevel mixed-effects robust linear model (RLM)—to account for the hierarchical structure of the dataset; and
e. Cluster-robust random-effects panel GLS—to model unobserved heterogeneity assuming exogeneity of moderators.

These estimators are applied to Eq. (4.3), using the three key regional indicators (East Asia, South Asia, and *SE*) along with the seven moderators identified in Sect. 5.2 via BMA and WALS. The results are presented in Table 5.3. A key pattern emerges: the estimated coefficients vary somewhat across estimators, reflecting differences in weighting and error structure. To address this, we adopt a conservative robustness rule—consistent with Iwasaki et al. (2020)—whereby a moderator is considered robust if it is statistically significant and maintains the same sign in at least three out of the five estimators.

Applying this rule, we find that East Asia consistently yields a negative and statistically significant coefficient across all estimators, indicating that the reported effects of financial development on growth are systematically weaker in East Asia compared to studies of the whole of Asia (our baseline category). In contrast, South Asia displays negative coefficients in all models but fails to reach statistical significance in any, suggesting that while the point estimates align directionally with the expected regional contrast, the evidence is less definitive. Overall, these patterns reinforce the meta-synthesis findings from Sect. 5.1 and lend additional support to Hypothesis 2, which posits that the finance–growth nexus is stronger in South Asia than in East Asia due to differences in baseline financial depth and developmental context.

Turning to the selected moderators, we find that market capitalization, financial market liberalization, and capital account openness consistently exhibit significant effects across models, with coefficients that are robust in both sign and significance. These variables appear to be key channels

Table 5.3 Meta-regression analysis with selected moderators

Estimator (Analytical weight in brackets)	*Cluster-robust WLS [1/SE]*	*Cluster-robust WLS [d.f.]*	*Cluster-robust WLS [1/EST]*	*Multi-level mixed-effects RLM*	*Cluster-robust random-effects panel GLS*
Meta-independent variable (Default)/ Model	*[1]*	*[2]*	*[3]*	*[4]*	*[5][a]*
Target region (Whole of Asia)					
East Asia	–0.1770***	–0.1117**	–0.0750	–0.1110**	–0.1061**
	(0.067)	(0.051)	(0.069)	(0.051)	(0.047)
South Asia	–0.1027	–0.0754	–0.0060	–0.0390	–0.0362
	(0.069)	(0.058)	(0.065)	(0.096)	(0.098)
Selected moderators					
Average year of estimation	–0.0093**	–0.0115**	–0.0088**	–0.0123***	–0.0125***
	(0.004)	(0.005)	(0.004)	(0.003)	(0.004)
Market capitalization	0.2542**	0.2778***	0.1060*	0.2521**	0.2524**
	(0.100)	(0.085)	(0.060)	(0.111)	(0.112)
Turnover ratio	–0.1731**	–0.0541	–0.2839	–0.2534**	–0.2559**
	a(0.069)	(0.075)	(0.225)	(0.112)	(0.113)
Capital account openness	–0.4446**	–0.3812**	–0.0747	–0.5185***	–0.5241***
	(0.174)	(0.163)	(0.110)	(0.174)	(0.174)
Financial market liberalization	–0.3770***	–0.2935***	–0.2522***	–0.4214***	–0.4251***
	(0.083)	(0.083)	(0.062)	(0.077)	(0.077)
Stock market liberalization	–0.3345**	–0.2374	–0.1503**	–0.4824***	–0.4861***
	(0.167)	(0.148)	(0.070)	(0.114)	(0.114)
Financial crisis	0.2155***	0.1722***	0.0817**	0.0727	0.0680
	(0.067)	(0.063)	(0.030)	(0.067)	(0.064)
SE	0.25749	0.22005	0.05838	–0.55941	–0.60337
	(0.4012)	(0.5871)	(0.4995)	(0.8545)	(0.8936)
Intercept	18.81614***	23.02403**	17.76379**	24.80391***	25.14872***
	(7.1546)	(9.4487)	(7.7912)	(7.0110)	(7.0140)
K	759	759	759	759	759
R^2	0.287	0.203	0.066	–	0.132

Notes figures in parentheses beneath the regression coefficients are robust standard errors. ***, **, and * denote statistical significance at the 1%, 5%, and 10% levels, respectively. Selected moderators denote meta-independent variables having a PIP of 0.50 or more in the Bayesian model averaging estimation and a *t* value of 1.96 or more in the WALS estimation as reported in Table 5.2. See Table 3.3 for the definitions and descriptive statistics of meta-independent variables.— = not applicable, *d.f.* = degrees of freedom, *EST* = number of estimates, GLS = generalized least squares, PIP = posterior inclusion probabilities, RLM = robust linear model, *SE* = standard error, WLS = weighted least squares

[a] Breusch-Pagan LM test for random effects: $\chi^2 = 9.92$, $p = 0.0008$

through which globalization and financial deepening influence growth outcomes in the region. The average year of estimation and turnover ratio also demonstrate consistent negative effects, indicating that more recent studies and those focusing on more liquid markets tend to report smaller effect sizes—perhaps reflecting greater methodological caution or post-crisis data environments.

By contrast, the variable capturing financial crises is positively associated with the effect size, and statistically significant in most models. This suggests that studies explicitly controlling for crisis episodes tend to find stronger finance–growth links—likely because crises amplify the visibility of financial sector dynamics. This interpretation aligns with the findings of Anwar and Cooray (2012), who noted that the Asian Financial Crisis had a disproportionate impact on the region, shaping subsequent research designs and estimates.

Interestingly, the remaining macroeconomic control variables—macroeconomic stability, trade openness, and investment—do not exert robust influence on reported effect sizes. This implies that these standard growth controls, while theoretically important, do not materially shift the empirical association between finance and growth once other moderators are included. These findings are consistent with the results in Table 5.2 and further validate the selection process used in the BMA and WALS frameworks.

In summary, the results in Table 5.3 show a high degree of consistency with the synthesis values reported earlier and reinforce the presence of robust subregional differences and financial drivers in the finance–growth–globalization nexus. They also demonstrate that the pattern of results is not an artifact of any single estimation method. Rather, the triangulated use of multiple estimators confirms the substantive conclusions drawn from the preceding analyses.

5.4 Globalization as a Moderator: Key Insights

The role of globalization in shaping the finance–growth relationship has long been a point of theoretical and empirical contention. While financial openness and liberalization are often associated with deeper capital markets, increased investment flows, and greater efficiency in resource allocation, they may also introduce volatility, crisis risk, and institutional vulnerabilities. The results of our MRA offer important new insights into how globalization-related factors—particularly capital account openness, financial liberalization, and financial crises—moderate the finance–growth nexus across Asian economies.

Three globalization variables—capital account openness, financial market liberalization, and stock market liberalization—emerge as consistently significant moderators in both the BMA/WALS selection procedure and the full MRA results in Table 5.3. Interestingly, all three carry negative coefficients, indicating that greater openness generally fails to enhance the positive association between finance and growth in the Asian context. This stands in contrast to conventional expectations and suggests that liberalization alone may be insufficient—if not counterproductive—without supportive institutions and safeguards.

Among these, capital account openness has the most stable and sizable negative effect. It is statistically significant in four out of five estimators and appears as a high-PIP variable in the BMA results. This finding echoes concerns raised in prior studies, such as those of Valickova et al. (2015), that capital mobility in emerging markets can exacerbate macroeconomic fragility when unaccompanied by adequate regulatory oversight. In Asia, several economies that liberalized their capital accounts during the 1990s subsequently experienced destabilizing capital outflows during periods of global financial turbulence—most notably during the 1997 Asian Financial Crisis and the 2008 global financial crisis.

Similarly, financial market liberalization and stock market liberalization both show robust negative effects. In five out of five MRA estimators for financial market liberalization, and in four out of five for stock market liberalization, the coefficients remain negative and statistically significant. These patterns suggest that, while liberalization may enhance market depth and participation, it can also induce volatility, speculative flows, and a disconnect between financial development and real-sector outcomes. Estrada et al. (2015) argue that in many parts of Asia, liberalization outpaced the development of financial infrastructure, leading to fragile capital markets unable to withstand external shocks or mispricing risks.

The negative moderating effects of these globalization proxies may also reflect heterogeneous timing and sequencing across countries. As Sharma and Kautish (2020) observe, financial liberalization in Asia often preceded institutional strengthening and regulatory harmonization. In such cases, openness may not improve allocative efficiency but instead amplify misalignments in credit and investment decisions, particularly when governance and transparency standards remain weak.

By contrast, the financial crisis variable exerts a positive and statistically significant effect on reported estimates. This counterintuitive result appears robust across at least three estimators, indicating that studies controlling for crisis episodes tend to report stronger and more significant estimates of the finance–growth relationship. One plausible interpretation is that crises serve as catalysts for reform: post-crisis periods often witness the implementation of macroprudential regulation, institutional restructuring, and the recapitalization of banking systems. These structural improvements may strengthen the finance–growth linkage in the aftermath of economic turmoil. For instance, Anwar and Cooray (2012) found that the impact of the Asian Financial Crisis was both regionally concentrated and temporally transformative—leading to long-term institutional changes that increased the effectiveness of financial development as a growth engine.

Taken together, the evidence suggests that globalization, when proxied by liberalization and openness variables, does not unconditionally strengthen the finance–growth relationship in Asia. Instead, it appears that the benefits of globalization are contingent upon the sequencing of reforms, regulatory capacity, and the maturity of domestic financial institutions. Where liberalization has been implemented in advance of these enabling conditions, the results have been uneven, and in some cases, counterproductive.

This finding reinforces the broader theoretical perspective that financial globalization is not a uniform process but a conditional driver—its effect shaped by context-specific institutional and macroeconomic environments (Rodrik & Subramanian, 2009). Moreover, the significant role of crisis episodes underscores that historical junctures matter. Liberalization may not yield growth dividends unless accompanied by durable institutional reforms, effective risk management systems, and policy buffers that mitigate external shocks.

In conclusion, our meta-regression findings suggest a nuanced and cautious view of globalization as a moderator. While openness and liberalization are widely promoted as policy imperatives, their growth-enhancing potential depends critically on context, capacity, and crisis responsiveness. These insights carry important implications for policymakers aiming to promote global financial integration in ways that preserve domestic economic resilience.

5.5 Subregional Divergence: South Asia Versus. East Asia

A core objective of this meta-analysis has been to assess whether the effects of financial development and globalization differ systematically across Asia's two principal subregions. Hypothesis 2 posits that the finance–growth relationship is stronger in South Asia than in East Asia, owing to contrasting institutional histories, financial structures, and development trajectories. Drawing on the cumulative evidence from synthesis, moderator selection, and robustness testing (Tables 5.1, 5.2, and 5.3), this section offers a contextual interpretation of the observed subregional asymmetries.

Across all layers of analysis, the results support the idea that finance contributes more robustly to growth in South Asia than in East Asia. Studies focused on South Asia tend to report stronger marginal effects of financial development, while those centered on East Asia yield systematically smaller estimates. This divergence is unlikely to be driven by sampling or publication bias alone; rather, it reflects meaningful differences in how finance interacts with economic structures and globalization processes in the two regions.

One critical explanatory factor is the nature and timing of financial globalization. As highlighted in Sect. 5.2, our moderator selection identifies capital account openness and stock market liberalization as significant but negatively signed influences on reported effect sizes. These channels are particularly relevant for East Asia, where rapid liberalization during the 1990s often outpaced institutional reform, exposing economies to destabilizing capital flows and speculative booms (Estrada et al., 2015). The post-crisis literature that followed tended to adopt more cautious conclusions, further dampening reported finance–growth effects in the region.

By contrast, South Asia has generally pursued a more incremental and domestically grounded approach to financial development. Financial globalization in this subregion has proceeded slowly and selectively, allowing for institutional adaptation and the sequencing of regulatory reforms. In particular, the expansion of financial access—via state-led banking outreach, microfinance, and digital inclusion—has played a central role in shaping the finance–growth dynamic. The robust positive role of market capitalization, as detected in both BMA and WALS models, is especially salient in this context, reflecting the growing influence of equity markets and digital finance in South Asia's financial transformation (Liu & Zhang, 2020; Anwar & Iwasaki, 2023a).

Baseline financial conditions also matter. In South Asia, historically low levels of financial penetration, especially in rural and informal sectors, imply that marginal improvements—such as SME credit, fintech-enabled lending, or public financial schemes—can yield disproportionately large economic benefits. These supply-side gains are particularly pronounced in economies like Bangladesh and India, where mobile banking and digital ID-linked systems (e.g., the JAM trinity) have expanded financial participation (Anwar & Cooray, 2012).

In contrast, many East Asian economies entered the period of analysis with already mature financial systems. Countries like South Korea, Malaysia, and Thailand were early adopters of financial liberalization, but the marginal growth effects of further deepening appear limited. Moreover, several East Asian economies have encountered rising debt burdens, household financial fragility, or regulatory saturation. The tighter macroprudential stance adopted after the 1997 Asian Financial Crisis, while stabilizing, may have constrained the developmental potential of additional financial flows. These structural ceilings help explain why the reported finance–growth links in East Asia remain modest, even when controlling for other factors.

Temporal patterns further illuminate these trends. As seen in Table 5.3, the average year of estimation is negatively associated with reported effect sizes, suggesting that newer studies tend to find weaker impacts. Since East Asia was more intensively studied in earlier phases—during post-crisis adjustment and liberalization—the region's estimates may reflect a historical ceiling on finance's marginal contribution. Meanwhile, the more recent emergence of South Asia-focused studies captures the effects of contemporary innovations and reforms, including mobile finance and public-private infrastructure financing.

Another dimension is the role of financial crises. The meta-regression results show that studies controlling for crisis events tend to report stronger finance–growth associations. This likely reflects the structural reforms and institutional modernization that often follow financial disruptions. While East Asia bore the brunt of the 1997 crisis and responded with substantial financial restructuring, these reforms have not always translated into stronger growth effects—possibly due to already high levels of financial intermediation and a shift toward stabilization over expansion.

In South Asia, by contrast, many economies were less directly affected by past crises. Their slower and steadier financial deepening has arguably avoided the pitfalls of volatility while delivering consistent, albeit modest, growth dividends. This contrast suggests that financial reforms that are inclusive, sequenced, and resilient to shocks are more likely to sustain long-term growth benefits.

In sum, the subregional divergence uncovered in this study reflects deeper asymmetries in financial architecture, globalization strategy, and development stage. South Asia reaps relatively higher returns from financial development, facilitated by digital inclusion and controlled liberalization. East Asia, while more financially advanced, faces diminishing returns and volatility risks from deeper integration. These findings reinforce the importance of tailoring financial sector strategies to institutional capacity, regulatory readiness, and the specific growth constraints of each region.

Notes

1. Regarding the evaluation criteria of the correlation coefficient, Cohen (1988) suggests using the values of 0.10, 0.30, and 0.50 as cutoffs to distinguish a small effect, medium effect, and large effect, respectively. However, his criteria set with a zero-order correlation are somewhat strict in economics research in which a large number of control variables are usually employed in empirical analysis. Therefore, Doucouliagos (2011) proposes 0.104, 0.226, and 0.386 to be the lowest thresholds of small, medium, and large effects, respectively, as the new general standard in macroeconomic research (ibid., Table 3.3, p. 11).
2. We further test the robustness of the main effects using moderator-enhanced MRA models. Supplementary meta-regression results and robustness checks are provided in Table A2.

CHAPTER 6

Publication Bias and the Credibility of Finance–Growth Evidence

6.1 Detecting and Diagnosing Publication Selection Bias

In the final stage of meta-analysis, we examine publication selection bias using a funnel plot, by conducting a goodness-of-fit test of proportional distribution and by performing an MRA test procedure consisting of a funnel-asymmetry test (FAT), a precision-effect test (PET), and a precision-effect estimate with standard error (PEESE), which are proposed by Stanley and Doucouliagos (2012) and have been used widely in recent meta-studies.

A funnel plot is a scatter plot with the effect size (in the case of this paper, the PCC) on the horizontal axis and the precision of the estimate (the inverse of the standard error $1/SE$) on the vertical axis. In the absence of publication selection bias, effect sizes reported by independent studies vary randomly and symmetrically around the true effect size. Moreover, according to statistical theory, the dispersion of effect sizes is negatively correlated with the precision of the estimate. Therefore, the shape of the plot should look like an inverted funnel. On the contrary, if the funnel plot is not symmetrical but rather is deflected to one side, then an arbitrary manipulation of the study area in question is suspected. In other words, the estimates in favor of a specific conclusion (i.e., estimates with an expected sign) are published more frequently.

A. Anwar, I. Iwasaki, *Meta-Analysis of Finance and Growth in Asia*,
https://doi.org/10.1007/978-3-032-10219-5_6

The goodness-of-fit test examines the proportional distribution of the reported estimates. The test is performed based on either the assumption that the true effect size is zero or the assumption that the selected meta-synthesis value approximates the true effect. By conducting this univariate test, we inspect whether the estimates in question are distributed evenly around the true effect size.

The FAT–PET–PEESE procedure has been developed to test publication selection bias and the presence of genuine evidence in a more rigid manner: FAT can be performed by regressing the t value of the k–th estimate on the inverse of the standard error ($1/SE$) using the next Eq. (6.1), thereby testing the null hypothesis that the intercept term γ_0 is equal to zero:

$$t_k = \gamma_0 + \gamma_1(1/SE_k) + v_k, \tag{6.1}$$

where v_k is the error term. When the intercept term γ_0 is statistically significantly different from zero, we can interpret that the distribution of the effect sizes is asymmetrical.

Even if there is publication selection bias, a genuine effect may exist in the available empirical evidence. Stanley and Doucouliagos (2012) propose examining this possibility by testing the null hypothesis that the coefficient γ_1 is equal to zero in Eq. (6.1). The rejection of the null hypothesis implies the presence of genuine empirical evidence. γ_1 is the coefficient of precision; therefore, it is called a PET.

Furthermore, Stanley and Doucouliagos (2012) also stated that an estimate of the publication selection bias–adjusted effect size can be obtained by estimating the following Eq. (6.2a), which has no intercept. If the null hypothesis of $\varphi_1 = 0$ is rejected, then the nonzero true effect does actually exist in the literature, and the coefficient φ_1 can be regarded as its estimate.

$$t_k = \varphi_0 SE_k + \varphi_1(1/SE_k) + w_k, \tag{6.2a}$$

where w_k is the error term. This is the PEESE approach.[1]

To test the robustness of the regression coefficients obtained from the above FAT–PET–PEESE procedure, we estimate Eqs. (6.1) and (6.2a) using not only the unrestricted WLS estimator, but also the WLS estimator with bootstrapped standard errors, the cluster-robust WLS estimator, and the unbalanced panel estimator for a robustness check. In addition to these four models, we also run an instrumental variable (IV) estimation with the inverse of the square root of the number of observations used as an instrument of the standard error, because "the standard error can be endogenous if some method choices affect both the estimate and the standard error. Moreover, the standard error is estimated, which causes attenuation bias in meta-analysis" (Cazachevici et al., 2020, p. 5).

Figure 6.1 Presents a funnel plot of the collected estimates. Panel (a), based on all 79 studies, exhibits an inverted funnel shape—consistent with random dispersion around the estimated effect size and suggesting that strong publication bias is unlikely. A similar shape appears in Panels (c) and

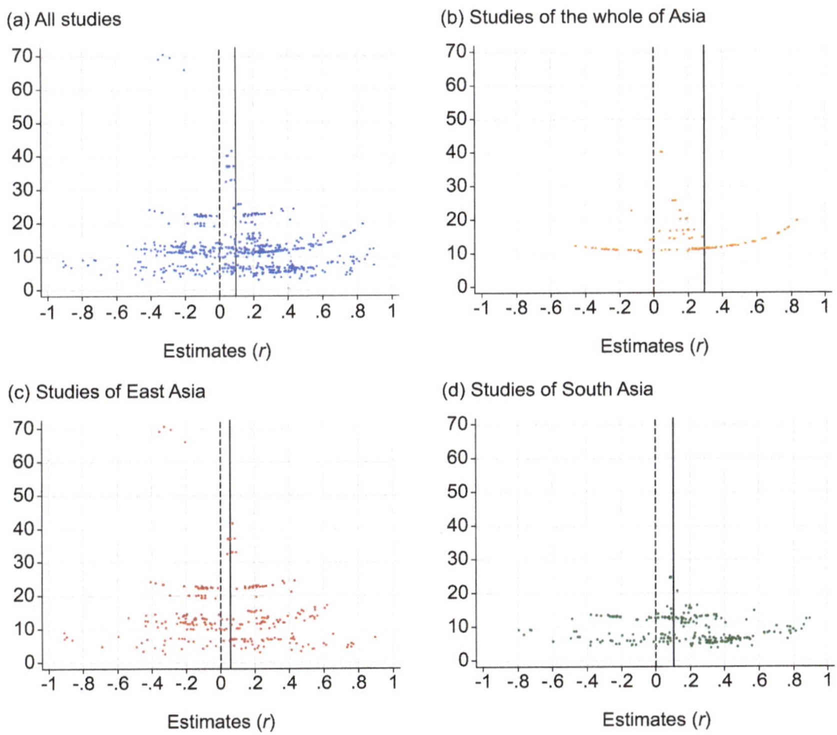

Fig. 6.1 Funnel plot of partial correlation coefficients. *Note* Solid line indicates the selected synthesis value as reported in Table 5.1

(d) for East Asia and South Asia, respectively. However, Panel (b), which focuses on studies of Asia as a whole, shows asymmetry skewed toward positive values, hinting at selective reporting in favor of expected outcomes

To support the findings obtained from the funnel plots in Fig. 6.1, we further examine whether the collected estimates are distributed proportionally around the true effect but not through a goodness-of-fit test. As shown in Table 6.1, the number of positive and negative estimates among those collected from all studies would be 528:231. This strongly rejects the null hypothesis that the true effect size is zero ($z = 10.780$, $p = 0.000$). The same information is also illustrated by the dotted line in Fig. 6.1. Furthermore, the selected synthesis value, as depicted by the solid line in Fig. 6.1, approximates the true effect; in this case, the collected estimates would be distributed more evenly (427:332) on the left and right sides of the threshold of 0.095. Nevertheless, the null hypothesis is again rejected ($z = 3.448$, $p = 0.001$). Similar test results are found in nearly all cases except for studies of East Asia under the assumption that the true effect size takes the random-effect synthesis value of 0.057.

As seen above, a visual examination using a funnel plot in Fig. 6.1 and the univariate test in Table 6.1 produced mutually contradictory results. Therefore, we will rely on the FAT–PET–PEESE procedure for a final judgment, as it is methodologically stricter. Results using estimates collected from all studies are shown in Table 6.2. As reported in Panel (a) of the table, in four of the five models, FAT rejects the null hypothesis that the intercept (γ_0) is zero. This suggests that publication selection bias in this research domain could be highly likely, in line with the goodness-of-fit test results in Table 6.1. However, even if publication selection bias is involved, the collected estimates could contain genuine empirical evidence. Panel (a) of Table 6.2 shows that the null hypothesis that the coefficient (γ_1) of the inverse of the standard error ($1/SE$) is zero is rejected in three models and, accordingly, proves that the collected estimates do contain empirical evidence regarding the true effect size. Further, the results of the PEESE approach in Panel (b) show that, in four models, the coefficients (φ_1) of $1/SE$ are statistically significant. For all studies combined, the publication bias–adjusted effect size is estimated to fall between 0.0598 and 0.0934 in terms of the PCC. These estimates suggest that the finance–growth relationship remains positive and economically meaningful in Asia, lending support to Hypothesis 1.

Table 6.1 Univariate test of publication selection bias

Study type	*Number of estimates (K)*	*Under the assumption that the true effect size is zero*			*Under the assumption that the true effect size is the selected synthesis value (x)*		
		Number of estimates		*Goodness-of-fit z test (p value)*[a]	*Number of estimates*		*Goodness-of-fit z test (p value)*[b]
		$PCC_k < 0$	$PCC_k > 0$		$PCC_k < x$	$PCC_k > x$	
All studies	759	231	528	10.780*** (0.000)	332	427	3.448*** (0.001)
Studies of the whole of Asia	160	35	125	0.294*** (0.000)	97	63	−2.688*** (0.007)
Studies of East Asia	332	140	192	2.854*** (0.004)	157	175	0.988 (0.323)
Studies of South Asia	267	56	211	9.486*** (0.000)	102	165	3.856*** (0.000)

Notes [a] Null hypothesis: the ratio of the positive to negative values is 50:50. [b] Null hypothesis: the ratio of estimates below *x* versus those over *x* is 50:50
*** denotes statistical significance at the 1% level

Table 6.2 Meta-regression analysis of publication selection: all studies

(a) FAT–PET test (Equation: $t = \gamma_0 + \gamma_1(1/SE) + v$)

Estimator	*Unrestricted WLS*	*WLS with bootstrapped standard errors*	*Cluster-robust WLS*	*Cluster-robust fixed-effects panel LSDV*	*IV*
Model	*[1]*	*[2]*	*[3]*	*[4]* [a]	*[5]*
Intercept (FAT: H_0: $\gamma_0 = 0$)	2.2128***	2.2128***	2.2128**	1.0438	1.6424***
	(0.549)	(0.507)	(1.066)	(2.173)	(0.348)
$1/SE$ (PET: H_0: $\gamma_1 = 0$)	0.0602***	0.0602***	0.0602	0.1948***	0.0155
	(0.017)	(0.014)	(0.092)	(0.047)	(0.025)
K	759	759	759	759	759
R^2	0.1988	0.0135	0.0135	0.0135	0.0061

(b) PEESE approach (Equation: $t = \varphi_0 SE + \varphi_1(1/SE) + w$)

Estimator	*Unrestricted WLS*	*WLS with bootstrapped standard errors*	*Cluster-robust WLS*	*Random-effects panel ML*	*IV*
Model	*[6]*	*[7]*	*[8]*	*[9]*	*[10]*
SE	7.8926***	7.8926***	7.8926*	0.9626	-24.8032***
	(2.177)	(1.976)	(4.116)	(2.957)	(7.296)
$1/SE$ (H_0: $\varphi_1 = 0$)	0.0598**	0.0598**	0.0598	0.0900*	0.0934***
	(0.026)	(0.025)	(0.125)	(0.052)	(0.019)
K	759	759	759	759	759
R^2	0.0791	0.0767	0.0791	–	–

Notes Figures in parentheses beneath the regression coefficients are standard errors. Models [3], [4], and [8] report standard errors clustered by study. Models [5] and [10] use the inverse of the square root of the number of observations as an instrument of the standard error

*** and ** denote statistical significance at the 1% and 5% levels, respectively

[a] Hausman test: $\chi 2 = 44.08$, $p = 0.0000$

Table 6.3 Summary of publication selection bias test

Study type	*Number of estimates (K)*	*Test results*[a]		
		Funnel asymmetry test (FAT) (H_0: γ_0 = 0)	*Precision-effect test (PET) (H_0: γ_1 = 0)*	*Precision-effect estimate with standard error (PEESE) (H_0: γ_1 = 0)*[b]
All studies	759	Rejected	Rejected	Rejected (0.0598/0.0934)
Studies of the whole of Asia	160	Not rejected	Rejected	Rejected (0.2618/0.2760)
Studies of East Asia	332	Rejected	Rejected	Rejected (0.0576)
Studies of South Asia	257	Rejected	Rejected	Rejected (0.1030/0.1231)

Notes [a] The null hypothesis is rejected when two or three models show a statistically significant estimate. Otherwise not rejected

[b] Figures in parentheses are PSB-adjusted estimates. If two estimates are reported, the left and right figures denote the minimum and maximum estimates, respectively

We also attempt the above FAT–PET–PEESE procedure separately by study type. Table 6.3 summarizes the results together with those for all studies mentioned above. As reported in this table, FAT identifies publication selection bias in two of the three cases. PET suggests the presence of genuine empirical evidence in all three cases, and the PEESE approach produces a publication selection–adjusted effect size that is statistically significantly different from zero for all three study types. The PEESE-generated values shown in the right-most column in Table 6.3 well conform to the meta-synthesis results as described in Sect. 5.1, thereby reconfirming that the financial systems in South Asia tend to outperform those in East Asia in terms of the growth-enhancing impact, as predicted in Hypothesis 2.[2]

6.2 Alternative Estimators and Bias-Corrected Effect Sizes

To verify the robustness of the FAT–PET–PEESE results, we apply four complementary techniques designed to correct for publication selection bias: the Top 10% method (Stanley et al., 2010), the selection model

(Andrews & Kasy, 2019), the endogenous kinked model (Bom & Rachinger, 2019), and the p-uniform approach (van Aert & van Assen, 2021). These models differ in how they address the probability of publication or the distribution of p-values, but share the aim of estimating a more credible underlying effect size. Table 6.4 presents the results obtained from all four methods across the full sample and regional subsamples.

Table 6.4 Alternative estimates of publication selection bias–corrected effect size

Method	*Top 10*[a]	*Selection model*[b]	*Endogeneous kinked model*[c]	*p-uniform*[d]
Model	*[1]*	*[2]*	*[3]*	*[4]*
(a) All studies				
Publication selection bias–corrected effect size	0.0528**	0.0910***	0.0465***	0.0602***
	(0.025)	(0.027)	(0.003)	(0.019)
K	75	759	759	759
(b) Studies of the whole of Asia				
Publication selection bias–corrected effect size	0.2825***	0.1560	0.2338***	0.1768***
	(0.084)	(0.044)	(0.073)	(0.006)
K	16	160	160	160
(c) Studies of East Asia				
Publication selection bias–corrected effect size	0.0219	0.0420	0.0710**	0.1021***
	(0.043)	(0.035)	(0.031)	(0.024)
K	33	332	332	332
(d) Studies of South Asia				
Publication selection bias–corrected effect size	0.0942*	0.0350*	0.0426	0.1226***
	(0.047)	(0.062)	(0.046)	(0.007)
K	26	267	267	267

Notes Figures in parentheses are standard errors

*** denotes that the coefficient is statistically significantly different from zero at the 1% level

[a] Arithmetic average of the top 10% most precise estimates (Stanley et al., 2010)

[b] Test for publication selection bias using the conditional probability of publication as a function of a study's results (Andrews & Kasy, 2019)

[c] Piecewise linear meta-regression of estimates on their standard errors, with a kink at the cutoff value of the standard error below which publication selection bias is unlikely (Bom & Rachinger, 2019)

[d] Method based on the statistical theory that the distribution of *p*-values is uniform conditional on the population effect size (van Aert & van Assen, 2021)

For the full sample, the bias-adjusted partial correlation coefficients (PCCs) range from 0.0465 (kinked model) to 0.0910 (selection model), closely aligning with the earlier PET and PEESE estimates (0.0598–0.0934). This convergence strengthens the credibility of the overall finance–growth relationship and supports the conclusion that, even after adjusting for selection bias, the effect remains positive and statistically meaningful.

Subregional estimates also align with expectations. In studies of the whole of Asia, corrected effects range from 0.1560 to 0.2825, indicating a moderate impact. For East Asia, adjusted estimates are lower (0.0219–0.1021), mirroring the weaker synthesis and regression results reported in Chap. 5. South Asia, by contrast, exhibits more stable and positive estimates—ranging from 0.0350 to 0.1226—again confirming the stronger finance–growth relationship in this region.

Taken together, these alternative estimates reinforce the core findings of the meta-regression and bias-correction analysis: financial development exerts a positive influence on growth in Asia, albeit with regional variation and sensitivity to publication dynamics. The convergence of results across multiple correction strategies strengthens confidence in the reliability of the literature and supports its use in evidence-based policy design.

6.3 What the Literature Gets Right—and What it Misses

After examining nearly 80 studies and over 750 effect size estimates, this meta-analysis arrives at a balanced yet cautiously optimistic conclusion: the literature on financial development and growth in Asia is generally credible, but not without flaws. On balance, most published estimates report a positive association between finance and growth—an association that remains statistically and economically meaningful even after correcting for potential biases in study selection and reporting.

Across multiple diagnostic tools—funnel plots, goodness-of-fit tests, and the FAT–PET–PEESE framework—we find evidence of mild publication selection bias. Some estimates are more likely to be published when they confirm theoretical expectations or yield statistically significant results. Yet this bias does not negate the presence of a genuine underlying effect. Our bias-corrected synthesis, using PET, PEESE, and four additional advanced estimators (Table 6.4), consistently places the true effect size between 0.046 and 0.093 for Asia as a whole. While small, these values are statistically significant and align closely with the WAAP meta-synthesis estimates discussed in Chap. 5. The core finding holds: financial development in Asia contributes positively to economic growth, though with considerable variation across regions and contexts.

At the subregional level, the credibility of the evidence also holds up. South Asia, in particular, displays consistent bias-adjusted effect sizes across all correction methods, reinforcing the interpretation that finance has played a more transformative role in this subregion. In East Asia, where publication bias is weaker and the literature is more established, the corrected effects are smaller—but not zero. This suggests that while the marginal gains from financial development may be tapering in mature systems, they have not disappeared entirely.

Still, the literature is lacking on several fronts. First, it tends to underreport null or negative results, especially in older studies. The asymmetry visible in the funnel plots, especially for studies of the whole of Asia, hints at selective reporting. Second, estimates tend to decline over time—a pattern captured by the negative moderator on the average year of estimation. This likely reflects improvements in empirical methods, access to better data, and growing publication of more cautious or nuanced results.

Moreover, much of the earlier literature has treated financial liberalization as an unequivocal good. Our analysis suggests otherwise. Globalization-related variables such as capital account openness and stock market liberalization often weaken the finance–growth link—especially when liberalization outpaces regulatory capacity. This underscores a key point: financial development is not inherently beneficial; its impact depends on context, timing, and the sequencing of reforms.

In sum, the Asian finance–growth literature mostly gets the big picture right—finance matters—but often misses the subtleties. It overstates effects in some settings, underexplores heterogeneity, and occasionally allows theory to outrun evidence. Yet when viewed through the lens of robust meta-analysis, a more balanced and credible narrative emerges—one that offers a reliable basis for future research and policy.

Notes

1. We can see that the coefficient φ_1 in Eq. (6.2a) may become the estimate of the publication bias–adjusted effect size in light of the fact that the following equation is obtained when both sides of Eq. (6.2a) are multiplied by the standard error:

$$Effect_k = \varphi_0 SE_k^2 + \varphi_1 + w_k. \tag{6.2b}$$

   When directly estimating Eq. (6.2b), the WLS method, with $1/SE_k^2$ as the analytical weight, is used.
2. As Table 6.3 shows, it is noteworthy that, in most cases, the publication selection bias–adjusted effect sizes generated by the PEESE method are much closer to the WAAP synthesis values than to the random-effects values reported in Table 5.1. These results support the statement by Stanley et al. (2017) that, as compared with the traditional random-effects model, the WAAP is a more effective synthesis approach in the presence of publication selection bias.

CHAPTER 7

Conclusion—Rethinking Financial Development in an Interconnected Asia

As debates about the role of finance in economic development continue to evolve, this study has sought to provide a more structured, comparative, and empirically grounded understanding of the finance–growth nexus in Asia. By synthesizing evidence from 79 studies and more than 750 effect sizes, and by systematically addressing methodological heterogeneity and publication selection bias, this meta-analysis offers a reassessment of where and how financial development contributes to economic growth across the region. The findings speak to both the promise and the complexity of finance in an interconnected Asia: while the overall relationship remains positive and statistically robust, its strength and reliability vary markedly by subregion, by the nature of financial globalization, and by the methodological choices of individual studies. This concluding chapter distills the study's main insights, reflects on their implications for regional policy and financial reform, and outlines directions for future research.

7.1 Summary of Findings: Synthesis, Heterogeneity, and Credibility

This book set out to answer a fundamental question: How reliably does financial development contribute to economic growth in Asia, and under what conditions? This structured meta-analysis of 79 empirical

A. Anwar, I. Iwasaki, *Meta-Analysis of Finance and Growth in Asia*, https://doi.org/10.1007/978-3-032-10219-5_7

studies and 759 effect-size estimates investigates the relationship across diverse contexts, methodological approaches, and regional settings. The findings paint a cautiously optimistic picture—one that validates much of the existing literature, while also revealing where its claims need tempering and where policy nuance is essential.

At the most basic level, the results confirm that financial development—whether measured by credit depth, market capitalization, or financial liberalization—is positively associated with economic growth in Asia. The average effect, summarized through multiple synthesis techniques, is modest but statistically significant. This holds even after adjusting for the well-known challenge of publication selection bias. In other words, the finance–growth link remains visible and meaningful even when correcting for the tendency of journals to favor studies that report large, significant results.

But this topline conclusion masks considerable complexity underneath. A major theme to emerge from the analysis is heterogeneity—not every study reports the same effect, and not all contexts yield equal results. Some of this variation is expected: differences in data, estimation methods, and time periods naturally produce variation in reported outcomes. However, our meta-regression analysis shows that this variation is not random—it can be systematically explained by study-level characteristics such as region, financial indicator, degree of openness, and sample timing.

Three patterns stand out. First, the choice of financial variable matters. Among the many indicators used in the literature, market capitalization consistently exhibits a stronger positive association with growth. This suggests that deep, equity-based financial systems may be particularly effective at channeling funds to productive uses, especially in emerging markets with expanding investor bases. In contrast, measures of liberalization—especially capital account openness and stock market deregulation—tend to dampen the finance–growth link. While liberalization is often promoted as a path to efficiency, our results suggest that without strong regulatory institutions and sequencing of reforms, it can introduce volatility that undermines growth.

Second, regional context plays a decisive role. South Asia shows stronger and more consistent growth payoffs from financial development than East Asia. In part, this reflects differing baselines: South Asia began with more constrained financial systems, so marginal improvements—like credit access, digital inclusion, or SME financing—had larger impacts. East Asia, by contrast, already had more developed systems, and further expansion often brought diminishing returns or new risks. Additionally, East Asia's deeper integration into global financial markets meant greater exposure to external shocks, especially when liberalization outpaced institutional readiness.

Third, time matters. The average year of estimation has a negative association with reported effect sizes, suggesting that more recent studies tend to report smaller, more cautious effects. This likely reflects improvements in empirical methods, better data, and a greater willingness to publish null or mixed findings in recent years. It also means that earlier literature may have overstated the finance–growth relationship—intentionally or otherwise—due to methodological optimism or selective reporting.

These issues of credibility and bias were explored in depth in Chap. 6. Using visual (funnel plots), statistical (goodness-of-fit tests), and regression-based diagnostics (FAT–PET–PEESE), we identified moderate publication selection bias in the literature. However, when adjusting for this bias using five different estimation strategies—including newer approaches like the selection model and the p-uniform method—the core conclusion remained intact: financial development has a positive and statistically meaningful effect on growth, particularly when viewed in regional and methodological context.

In short, the literature largely gets the broad direction right, but often misses the nuance. Financial development can promote growth, but not uniformly and not unconditionally. The strength of the relationship depends on which aspect of finance is being measured, how open the economy is, and where and when the study is conducted. Our analysis underscores the importance of looking beyond average effects and toward patterns of heterogeneity and context.

This summary of findings offers two takeaways for future research and policymaking. First, one-size-fits-all narratives about finance and growth should be treated with caution. The diversity of outcomes across studies—and the ability to explain them through observable characteristics—suggests that tailoring financial policy to institutional capacity, reform history, and regional context is essential. Second, while the literature is generally credible, it still benefits from methodological refinement. Biases in publication, sample composition, and study design remain, but meta-analytic techniques provide tools to diagnose and correct for these issues.

What emerges from this study is not a single headline effect, but a structured framework for thinking about when and how finance supports growth. It is a message of qualified confidence—finance matters, but not always, not everywhere, and not in the same way. Recognizing that complexity is essential to both advancing the literature and designing financial systems that can effectively support inclusive and sustainable growth across an interconnected Asia.

These patterns suggest three implications for regional financial policy: (i) there is a reliable, positive average effect of finance on growth; (ii) this effect depends critically on institutions, reform timing, and market structure; and (iii) financial policy must be regionally tailored, particularly in response to the risks posed by premature liberalization or overreliance on external capital flows.

7.2 Translating Evidence into Regional Financial Policy

This study provides strong, empirically grounded support for the idea that financial development continues to matter for economic growth in Asia—but not uniformly, and not always in the ways conventionally assumed. One of the key contributions of this meta-analysis is its ability to unpack these effects with regional nuance and methodological transparency. The challenge now lies in translating these findings into financial policy frameworks that are better suited to Asia's economic diversity and evolving integration into the global economy.

At a broad level, the evidence confirms a small but statistically meaningful positive link between financial development and growth across the region. This association holds up across estimation strategies and remains robust even after accounting for publication bias. However, the relationship is highly conditional—mediated by the level of financial maturity, the degree of openness to global capital flows, and the sequencing of domestic reforms. Financial development, in other words, is neither universally beneficial nor automatically growth-enhancing. Its effectiveness depends on where a country starts, how reforms are implemented, and what institutional capacities exist to manage risk and direct finance to productive uses. These findings have particular relevance for finance ministries, regulatory agencies, and regional development institutions tasked with designing or evaluating financial sector reforms.

For South Asia, the results are particularly encouraging. The analysis reveals consistently stronger marginal effects of finance on growth in countries like India, Bangladesh, and Pakistan, where financial systems are still evolving and access to formal finance remains uneven. In these settings, policy should focus on deepening inclusion, expanding credit access for

SMEs, and strengthening regulatory frameworks that support innovation without sacrificing stability. The success of mobile banking platforms, digital identity systems, and targeted credit programs in several South Asian economies illustrates how incremental reforms can yield sizable returns when anchored in developmental priorities.

East Asia, by contrast, presents a more complex picture. While financial systems in this subregion are more mature and capital markets deeper, the growth effects of additional financial liberalization appear to be weaker and less consistent. In part, this reflects the region's earlier exposure to global capital flows, which—without sufficient institutional safeguards—contributed to volatility and crisis episodes, notably in 1997 and 2008. Going forward, East Asian policymakers may need to focus less on expanding financial depth and more on improving allocative efficiency, regulatory responsiveness, and risk management capacity. Strengthening macroprudential tools, enhancing transparency in bond and equity markets, and tightening the links between finance and the real economy could help revive the developmental role of finance in this more advanced regional context.

The findings on globalization-related variables reinforce this need for caution and context-specific planning. Capital account openness, stock market liberalization, and financial market deregulation are all associated with weaker finance–growth effects in the aggregate. This does not imply that liberalization is inherently harmful, but it does suggest that without prior institutional strengthening, liberalization can undercut stability and fail to deliver growth. As such, Asian economies should adopt a "sequencing-first" approach—ensuring that supervisory frameworks, governance standards, and financial literacy are in place before lifting capital controls or opening markets too rapidly.

Another insight from this study is the evolving nature of financial development's impact over time. More recent studies tend to report smaller effect sizes, likely reflecting both improvements in empirical methodology and changing macrofinancial conditions. Policymakers should therefore resist the temptation to anchor financial strategy to historical averages or stylized facts. Instead, they should engage more directly with up–to-date evidence, particularly that which reflects post-crisis reforms, digital transformations, and emerging financial risks.

Finally, the presence of statistically significant effects even after adjusting for publication bias suggests that the finance–growth literature, while imperfect, remains a useful guide for policy. That said, reliance on published estimates alone may be misleading if not critically interpreted.

Policymakers, especially in lower-income or institutionally constrained contexts, must approach finance-driven growth models with careful attention to context, sequence, and absorptive capacity.

In short, the findings of this meta-analysis call for a more targeted and adaptive approach to financial policy in Asia. Financial development should be treated not as a universal prescription, but as a policy lever whose effectiveness depends on the interaction of domestic institutions, reform timing, and external integration. Regional diversity is not a constraint—it is the foundation on which smarter, more resilient financial strategies must be built.

7.3 Rethinking Reform: Institutions, Timing, and Financial Design

This meta-analysis offers more than a verdict on whether finance supports growth in Asia—it opens a deeper conversation about how, when, and under what conditions financial development can best serve economic transformation. The results presented in earlier chapters point to a simple truth: financial liberalization and development do not operate in a vacuum. Their growth-enhancing potential is shaped—and often constrained—by institutional quality, reform sequencing, and the underlying design of financial systems. Understanding these interdependencies is critical to rethinking financial reform in an interconnected Asia.

A central insight from the meta-regression and publication bias analysis is that openness, on its own, is not a panacea. Variables capturing capital account openness and stock market liberalization consistently emerged as negative moderators across both the BMA/WALS selection process and the multivariate regressions (Tables 5.2 and 5.3). While conventional theory often links liberalization with efficiency and deeper market integration, the empirical evidence here suggests a more cautionary tale—especially in emerging Asian contexts where institutional capacity and financial oversight have not always kept pace with policy ambition.

As Estrada et al. (2015) note, many East Asian countries liberalized their financial systems rapidly in the 1990s without parallel investment in regulatory institutions. The aftermath was visible in the 1997 Asian Financial Crisis, and the long shadow of this episode is still evident in the data: countries with early, fast-paced reforms tend to report lower marginal effects of financial development on growth. This points to the critical importance of reform timing and institutional readiness. When liberalization precedes the development of prudential regulation, credit infrastructure, or transparency frameworks, the result is often heightened volatility rather than sustained growth.

In practical terms, this calls for targeted institutional development that supports financial resilience and productive transformation. Robust, independent, and well-capitalized central banks are essential for managing liquidity, anchoring inflation expectations, and responding credibly to financial shocks. Equally important are transparent and accountable regulatory authorities that oversee equity and bond markets, ensuring that financial deepening does not come at the expense of stability or investor confidence. In the digital age, regulatory focus must also extend to infrastructure—especially the platforms that enable mobile banking, digital payments, and biometric verification—since these systems now serve as the frontline of financial inclusion in much of Asia. Finally, financial systems must be equipped with credible crisis-resolution mechanisms, including deposit insurance schemes and macroprudential tools, that can mitigate contagion risks and preserve institutional trust during periods of external or domestic stress.

In contrast, the experience of South Asia offers a more gradualist and often more productive alternative. The finance–growth relationship is stronger in this subregion, even after correcting for potential publication bias (Chap. 6, Table 6.3). Countries such as India, Bangladesh, and Pakistan have approached financial opening more conservatively, often emphasizing access and stability over rapid integration. Initiatives like India's Jan Dhan-Aadhaar-Mobile (JAM) trinity and Bangladesh's microfinance sector exemplify reforms that expand financial inclusion while maintaining systemic resilience (Anwar & Cooray, 2012; Liu & Zhang, 2020). Here, reforms have been embedded in local institutional realities and tied to tangible development goals—an approach that appears to deliver more consistent growth dividends.

Another dimension is the design of financial systems themselves. The strong positive role of market capitalization as a moderator (Table 5.3) suggests that equity markets—when well-regulated—can channel resources effectively and stimulate investment. However, turnover ratios were found to have negative effects, implying that excess liquidity or speculative trading can undermine the development function of capital markets. The challenge for policymakers is to strike a balance between promoting market depth and curbing destabilizing dynamics. In this regard, financial design is not just about creating markets but ensuring they serve productive ends.

The publication selection bias–adjusted estimates (Table 6.4) further reinforce the credibility of these patterns. After correcting for systematic bias in the literature, the effect of financial development on growth remains positive but modest. This strengthens the argument for "smart" financial reform—not one-size-fits-all liberalization, but context-aware, sequenced, and institutionally grounded policy. Reform should be framed not around abstract targets for openness or credit ratios but around diagnostics of what impedes finance from supporting productive transformation —whether that is lack of access, weak enforcement, or poor crisis management tools.

In sum, the finance–growth literature in Asia offers a useful set of lessons, but only if read with an eye to nuance. Rapid liberalization without preparation may undercut development. Financial access without supporting infrastructure may deepen inequality. Reform without sequencing may fail to take root. A new generation of financial policy must therefore be more empirical, more contextual, and more grounded in how finance actually works, not just in theory, but on the ground. That is the task that follows from the findings of this book.

7.4 Limitations and Future Research Directions

While this meta-analysis offers robust and policy-relevant insights into the finance–growth relationship in Asia, it is important to acknowledge its limitations and identify paths for future research. Meta-analysis, by design, builds on published evidence—it systematizes rather than generates primary data. Accordingly, the quality and scope of its conclusions are shaped by the underlying literature it synthesizes. This chapter outlines three key limitations of the present study, followed by a research agenda that addresses these gaps and offers a roadmap for scholars and institutions exploring financial development in an interconnected Asia.

First, although this study provides a comprehensive review of nearly 80 empirical studies and more than 750 effect size estimates, the literature itself is uneven in quality, coverage, and design. Some subregions—particularly South Asia—have only recently seen a surge in finance–growth research, often with narrower samples or less variation in econometric techniques. Conversely, the literature on East Asia is more established but also more concentrated in post-crisis periods and earlier liberalization phases. This asymmetry affects not only the distribution of estimates but also the confidence with which subregional comparisons can be drawn.

Second, the meta-analysis is limited by the level of detail reported in primary studies. Many estimates lack full transparency about estimation methods, control variables, or robustness checks, which restricts the granularity of moderator coding. While our study applies rigorous selection criteria and advanced techniques like BMA and WALS to isolate key drivers of heterogeneity, it still cannot fully account for unobserved variables or specification nuances embedded in the original studies.

Third, like most meta-studies, our framework assumes comparability of effect sizes across contexts. The use of partial correlation coefficients (PCCs) allows for unit-free synthesis, but it also abstracts away from institutional and country-specific dynamics that may condition the finance–growth link. For example, a PCC of 0.10 in Bangladesh may imply a fundamentally different policy environment than the same effect size in Malaysia. While we partially address this through subregional analysis and moderator variables, future research will need to explore context-specific mechanisms in greater detail.

These limitations notwithstanding, this study offers a strong platform for continued inquiry. Building on the findings presented in earlier chapters—especially the nuanced roles of financial liberalization, institutional design, and crisis responsiveness—we outline three broad questions for future research:

First, our analysis reveals that globalization-related factors such as capital account openness and stock market liberalization tend to weaken the finance–growth relationship in Asia, particularly when introduced before robust regulatory infrastructure is in place (Estrada et al., 2015; Sharma & Kautish, 2020). Future research should disaggregate the liberalization-growth nexus further: Which forms of openness (e.g., FDI, portfolio, cross-border lending) are most growth-enhancing? Does sequencing—liberalization before versus after banking reforms—matter? Comparative country studies and multicountry panel analyses could clarify how timing, scope, and institutional preconditions influence outcomes.

Second, the results for South Asia suggest that digital financial tools—mobile banking, biometric ID-linked accounts, microfinance—can meaningfully expand financial access and yield positive growth dividends (Anwar & Cooray, 2012; Liu & Zhang, 2020). Yet few studies systematically examine the interaction between digital inclusion and macroeconomic performance. Future work should assess whether fintech-led development differs from traditional banking expansion in its growth implications. New datasets that track usage, credit access, and financial literacy across populations would enrich our understanding of inclusive finance as a growth driver.

Third, the positive and significant role of financial crisis as a moderator in our meta-regression suggests that post-crisis reform eras—particularly in East Asia—have reshaped financial institutions and their impact on growth. But are these effects durable? Do countries that liberalize after crises experience more stable finance–growth trajectories than those that liberalize during booms? Future research could exploit natural experiments and long panels to investigate how crisis legacies influence institutional evolution, financial architecture, and macrofinancial resilience.

Finally, while this study focused on published estimates, there is scope for expanding the meta-analytic base to include more grey literature, institutional reports, and working papers—particularly from underrepresented countries. Greater openness in data sharing and methodological transparency would also help future meta-analysts trace not only what results are reported but how they were generated.

In conclusion, this book has shown that financial development does matter for growth in Asia—but how, how much, and under what conditions remains a moving target. By placing evidence in context and identifying both strengths and blind spots in the literature, this study provides a foundation for smarter research and more adaptive policy. As Asia's economies continue to evolve—digitally, institutionally, and globally—the need for interdisciplinary, data-driven financial research will only grow. This volume invites researchers, policymakers, and institutions to join that journey.

For policymakers and financial institutions, the task ahead is clear. Financial development remains a powerful—but conditional—driver of growth. Its success depends not only on depth or liberalization, but on fit: fit with institutions, with capabilities, and with the region's stage of development. Moving forward, reforms must be empirically grounded, contextually sensitive, and resilience-focused. This book provides not only evidence but a framework to begin that work.

List of Appendices

Appendix A: Supplementary Tables A1 and A2

Table A1 List of 79 selected studies on finance and growth in Asia for meta-analysis

Author(s) (publication year)	*Target area*			*Estimation period*		*Number of collected estimates*
	Whole of Asia	*East Asia*	*South and inner Asia*	*From*	*To*	
Siddiki (2002)			✓	1975	1995	1
Fuchs-Schundeln and Funke (2003)	✓			1975	2000	14
Christopoulos and Tsionas (2004)			✓	1970	2000	1
Fink et al. (2005)		✓		1990	2001	1
Khan et al. (2005)			✓	1971	2004	2
Lee and Wong (2005)		✓		1965	2002	7

(continued)

A. Anwar, I. Iwasaki, *Meta-Analysis of Finance and Growth in Asia*,
https://doi.org/10.1007/978-3-032-10219-5

Table A1 (continued)

Author(s) (publication year)	*Target area*			*Estimation period*		*Number of collected estimates*
	Whole of Asia	*East Asia*	*South and inner Asia*	*From*	*To*	
Rousseau and Vuthipadadorn (2005)		✓	✓	1950	2000	30
Habibullah and Eng (2006)	✓			1990	1998	3
Liu and Hsu (2006)		✓		1981	2001	17
Padoan and Mariani (2006)		✓		1960	2001	12
Bussière and Fratzscher (2008)		✓		1980	2002	6
Guaiglia and Poncet (2008)		✓		1989	2003	9
Lee and Shin (2008)	✓			1980	1999	1
Ma and Jalil (2008)		✓	✓	1960	2006	4
Yang and Yi (2008)		✓		1971	2002	3
Gamra (2009)	✓			1980	2002	119
Hasan et al. (2009)		✓		1986	2002	30
Lee and Chang (2009)			✓	1970	2002	11
Lu and Yao (2009)		✓		1991	2001	6
Wadud (2009)			✓	1976	2008	1
Ang (2010)			✓	1966	2005	14
Chang and Huang (2010)		✓		1981	2008	26
Chiou-Wei et al. (2010)		✓		1970	2004	7
Dawson (2010)			✓	1960	2002	7
Hou and Cheng (2010)			✓	1971	2007	6
Jalil et al. (2010)		✓		1977	2006	2
Yao (2010)		✓		2002	2006	16

(continued)

Table A1 (continued)

Author(s) (publication year)	*Target area*			*Estimation period*		*Number of collected estimates*
	Whole of Asia	*East Asia*	*South and inner Asia*	*From*	*To*	
Anwar and Nguyen (2011)			✓	1997	2006	4
Hassan et al. (2011)		✓	✓	1980	2007	6
Jalil and Feridun (2011)			✓	1975	2008	2
Anwar and Cooray (2012)			✓	1970	2009	19
Horng et al. (2012)		✓		1961	2006	1
Zhang et al. (2012)		✓		2001	2006	19
Hye and Wizarat (2013)			✓	1971	2007	2
Narayan and Narayan (2013)	✓			1995	2011	3
Bayar (2014)	✓			1992	2011	7
Jahfer and Inoue (2014)			✓	1996	2011	4
Murthy et al. (2014)			✓	1971	2012	2
Nain and Kamaiah (2014)			✓	1990	2010	1
Peng et al. (2014)			✓	1978	2004	3
Sahoo (2014)			✓	1982	2012	16
Shahbaz and Rahman (2014)			✓	1991	2012	2
Sheera and Ashwani (2014)			✓	1999	2009	2
Lenka (2015)			✓	1980	2011	2
Mansury and Sohn (2015)			✓	1994	2007	5
Badeeb et al. (2016)			✓	1970	2013	4
Nyasha and Odhiambo (2016)		✓		1980	2012	4

(continued)

Table A1 (continued)

Author(s) (publication year)	*Target area*			*Estimation period*		*Number of collected estimates*
	Whole of Asia	*East Asia*	*South and inner Asia*	*From*	*To*	
Zhang and Bezemer (2016)		✓		1995	2013	12
Dai et al. (2017)		✓		1980	2012	2
Murari (2017)			✓	1980	2013	8
Ohlan (2017)			✓	1960	2014	2
Soedarmono et al. (2017)			✓	2000	2009	8
Williams (2017)	✓			1982	2011	1
Chung et al. (2019)			✓	1980	2012	30
Eren et al. (2019)		✓		1971	2015	2
Malarvizhi et al. (2019)			✓	1980	2011	9
Mohanty and Bhanumurthy (2019)			✓	1980	2016	4
Naveed and Mahmood (2019)			✓	1972	2010	2
Nawaz et al. (2019)			✓	1972	2017	2
Wang et al. (2019a)			✓	1989	2017	3
Wang et al. (2019b)		✓		2007	2016	4
Haini (2020)			✓	1995	2017	8
Jehan and Irshad (2020)			✓	1980	2016	4
Lenka and Sharma (2020)			✓	1980	2017	12
Liu and Zhang (2020)		✓		1996	2013	120
Rahman et al. (2020)			✓	1980	2017	2
Sharma and Kautish (2020)			✓	1990	2016	4

(continued)

Table A1 (continued)

Author(s) (publication year)	*Target area*			*Estimation period*		*Number of collected estimates*
	Whole of Asia	*East Asia*	*South and inner Asia*	*From*	*To*	
Muhammad et al. (2021)			✓	2000	2016	4
Nazir et al. (2021)		✓	✓	1970	2016	12
Siddikee and Rahman (2021)			✓	1990	2018	2
Yousaf et al. (2021)			✓	1972	2016	6
Arif et al. (2022)			✓	1980	2018	3
Verma and Giri (2022)			✓	2000	2017	2
Alhassan et al. (2023)	✓			1980	2017	12
Hossin (2023)			✓	1980	2014	4
Huo et al. (2023)		✓		1977	2021	2
Ren and Wu (2023)		✓		2004	2019	4
Usman (2023)		✓		1992	2021	1
Ye et al. (2023)		✓		2001	2016	4

Note Appendix B provides a detailed bibliography of the 79 studies listed in this table

Table A2 Meta-regression analysis with all moderators

Estimator (analytical weight in brackets)	*Cluster-robust WLS [1/SE]*	*Cluster-robust WLS [d.f.]*	*Cluster-robust WLS [1/EST]*	*Multilevel mixed -effects RML*	*Cluster-robust random-effects panel GLS*
Meta-independent variable (default)/model	*[1]*	*[2]*	*[3]*	*[4]*	*[5][a]*
Target region (whole of Asia)					
East Asia	−0.2723***	−0.1684	−0.3057***	−0.1213**	−0.1336
	(0.080)	(0.112)	(0.066)	(0.052)	(0.088)
South Asia	−0.2135**	−0.1654	−0.1800**	−0.0807	−0.0869
	(0.089)	(0.112)	(0.072)	(0.107)	(0.108)
Composition of target countries					
Number of target countries	−0.0009	−0.0006	−0.0029	0.0013	0.0012
	(0.003)	(0.003)	(0.002)	(0.003)	(0.003)
Share of developed countries	−0.0570	−0.0161	0.1969*	−0.0847	−0.0771
	(0.095)	(0.100)	(0.115)	(0.122)	(0.123)
Estimation period					
Average year of estimation	−0.0077*	−0.0039	−0.0082*	−0.0118**	−0.0115**
	(0.005)	(0.004)	(0.005)	(0.005)	(0.005)
Length of estimation	−0.0021	0.0008	−0.0040	−0.0016	−0.0017
	(0.003)	(0.003)	(0.003)	(0.003)	(0.003)
Data type (panel data)					
Cross−sectional data	0.0573	0.0633	0.0927	0.0663	0.0603
	(0.090)	(0.070)	(0.202)	(0.078)	(0.082)
Time−series data	0.1936	0.0833	0.1678*	0.1608	0.1609
	(0.126)	(0.133)	(0.099)	(0.130)	(0.130)
Estimator (estimators other than OLS)					
OLS	0.0550*	0.0110	0.2321***	0.0572**	0.0608**
	(0.033)	(0.027)	(0.053)	(0.026)	(0.028)

(continued)

Table A2 (continued)

Estimator (analytical weight in brackets)	*Cluster-robust WLS [1/SE]*	*Cluster-robust WLS [d.f.]*	*Cluster-robust WLS [1/EST]*	*Multilevel mixed -effects RML*	*Cluster-robust random-effects panel GLS*
Meta-independent variable (default)/model	*[1]*	*[2]*	*[3]*	*[4]*	*[5][a]*
Unit of growth variable (GDP per capita)					
Real GDP	−0.0720	−0.0429	−0.1677**	−0.0893	−0.0899
	(0.061)	(0.074)	(0.067)	(0.073)	(0.073)
Nominal GDP	−0.1677	−0.1428	0.1860	0.0006	−0.0042
	(0.149)	(0.152)	(0.159)	(0.166)	(0.169)
Type of financial variable (private credit to GDP)					
Financial depth	0.0483	0.0806	0.1806*	−0.0455	−0.0396
	(0.082)	(0.085)	(0.092)	(0.053)	(0.054)
Bank credit to GDP	−0.1566**	−0.1374*	−0.0663	−0.0890	−0.0880
	(0.068)	(0.070)	(0.081)	(0.085)	(0.086)
Private credit to domestic credit	−0.0253	0.0513	0.0546	−0.0682	−0.0643
	(0.070)	(0.076)	(0.090)	(0.053)	(0.055)
Market capitalization	0.1817**	0.2145***	0.1198	0.1774**	0.1822**
	(0.081)	(0.076)	(0.082)	(0.072)	(0.075)
Stock market activity	0.0480	0.1198	0.0887	0.0146	0.0171
	(0.093)	(0.093)	(0.089)	(0.114)	(0.116)
Turnover ratio	−0.2050***	−0.0854	−0.2755	−0.2714**	−0.2672**
	(0.075)	(0.097)	(0.203)	(0.114)	(0.115)
Comprehensive FD index	−0.1190	−0.1158	0.1661*	−0.1120	−0.1057
	(0.107)	(0.096)	(0.097)	(0.127)	(0.127)
Other FD variables	−0.2118***	−0.2074***	0.2640*	−0.2021**	−0.1921*
	(0.065)	(0.058)	(0.144)	(0.098)	(0.101)
Capital account openness	−0.4549**	−0.3936*	0.0265	−0.5257***	−0.5175***
	(0.204)	(0.209)	(0.121)	(0.187)	(0.193)

(continued)

Table A2 (continued)

Estimator (analytical weight in brackets)	*Cluster-robust WLS [1/SE]*	*Cluster-robust WLS [d.f.]*	*Cluster-robust WLS [1/EST]*	*Multilevel mixed -effects RML*	*Cluster-robust random-effects panel GLS*
Meta-independent variable (default)/model	*[1]*	*[2]*	*[3]*	*[4]*	*[5]*[a]
Financial market liberalization	−0.4012***	−0.3119***	−0.2381**	−0.4417***	−0.4367***
	(0.088)	(0.114)	(0.108)	(0.073)	(0.075)
Stock market liberalization	−0.3840**	−0.2470	−0.2218**	−0.4943***	−0.4892***
	(0.167)	(0.216)	(0.097)	(0.111)	(0.116)
Comprehensive FL index	−0.0964	−0.1355	0.2826*	−0.0456	−0.0432
	(0.113)	(0.116)	(0.143)	(0.113)	(0.114)
Other FL variables	0.1472	0.1749	0.0653	0.3353***	0.3367***
	(0.136)	(0.147)	(0.128)	(0.064)	(0.066)
Other characteristics of the financial variable					
Lagged	−0.0914	−0.0776	−0.1512*	−0.0981	−0.0968
	(0.098)	(0.126)	(0.078)	(0.082)	(0.082)
With intercepted variable	−0.0018	−0.0432	0.0644	−0.0208	−0.0162
	(0.045)	(0.031)	(0.065)	(0.038)	(0.039)
Selection of control variables					
Macroeconomic stability	−0.0061	−0.0177	0.0184	0.0085	0.0080
	(0.040)	(0.030)	(0.049)	(0.042)	(0.043)
Trade openness	0.0155	−0.0669	0.0449	0.0077	0.0089
	(0.056)	(0.066)	(0.055)	(0.052)	(0.054)
Investment	−0.0019	−0.0513	0.0454	0.0193	0.0241
	(0.042)	(0.053)	(0.057)	(0.041)	(0.043)
Financial crisis	0.1416**	0.0800	0.0373	0.0754	0.0811
	(0.060)	(0.058)	(0.064)	(0.056)	(0.061)
SE	−0.0695	0.4206	−0.5615	−0.7071	−0.6490
	(0.600)	(0.620)	(0.729)	(1.053)	(1.044)

(continued)

Table A2 (continued)

Estimator (analytical weight in brackets)	*Cluster-robust WLS [1/SE]*	*Cluster-robust WLS [d.f.]*	*Cluster-robust WLS [1/EST]*	*Multilevel mixed -effects RML*	*Cluster-robust random-effects panel GLS*
Meta-independent variable (default)/model	*[1]*	*[2]*	*[3]*	*[4]*	*[5]*[a]
Intercept	15.7418*	8.0917	16.7076*	23.9174**	23.3135**
	(9.059)	(8.639)	(9.831)	(9.360)	(9.662)
K	759	759	759	759	759
R^2	0.365	0.507	0.260	–	0.175

Notes Figures in parentheses beneath the regression coefficients are robust standard errors
***, **, and * denote statistical significance at the 1%, 5%, and 10% levels, respectively. See Table 3.3 for the definitions and descriptive statistics of meta-independent variables
[a]Breusch-Pagan LM test for random effects: $\chi^2 = 2.88$, $p = 0.0449$

Appendix B: Bibliography of the 79 Studies Included in the Meta-Analysis

Alhassan, A., Adamu, M. S., & Safiyanu, S. S. (2023). Finance-led growth hypothesis for Asia: An insight from new data. *Journal of the Asia Pacific Economy, 28*(2), 599–618.

Anwar, S., & Cooray, A. (2012). Financial development, political rights, civil liberties and economic growth: Evidence from South Asia. *Economic Modelling, 29*(3), 974–981.

Anwar, S., & Nguyen, L. P. (2011). Financial development and economic growth in Vietnam. *Journal of Economics and Finance, 35*(3), 348–360.

Arif, A., Sadiq, M., Shabbir, M. S., Yahya, G., Zamir, A., & Bares Lopez, L. (2022). The role of globalization in financial development, trade openness and sustainable environmental-economic growth: Evidence from selected South Asian economies. *Journal of Sustainable Finance & Investment, 12*(4), 1027–1044.

Badeeb, R. A., Lean, H. H., & Smyth, R. (2016). Oil curse and finance–growth nexus in Malaysia: The role of investment. *Energy Economics, 57*, 154–165.

Bayar, Y. (2014). Financial development and economic growth in emerging Asian countries. *Asian Social Science, 10*(9), 8–17.

Bussière, M., & Fratzscher, M. (2008). Financial openness and growth: Short-run gain, long-run pain? *Review of International Economics, 16* (1), 69–95.

Chang, S.-H., & Huang, L.-C. (2010). The nexus of finance and GDP growth in Japan: Do real interest rates matter? *Japan and the World Economy, 22*(4), 235–242.

Chiou-Wei, S. Z., Zhu, Z., & Wu, W.-C. (2010). Financial development and economic growth in South Korea: An application of smooth transition error correction analysis. *Applied Economics, 42*(16–18), 2041–2052.

Christopoulos, D. K., & Tsionas, E. G. (2004). Financial development and economic growth: Evidence from panel unit root and cointegration tests. *Journal of Development Economics, 73*(1), 55–74.

Chung, P. T., Sun, S., & Vo, D. T. H. (2019). How does financial development interact with economic growth in five ASEAN countries? *Singapore Economic Review, 64*(3), 441–460.

Dai, P. V., Delpachitra, S., & Cottrell, S. (2017). Real exchange rate and economic growth in East Asian countries: The role of financial integration. *Singapore Economic Review, 62*(1), 163–177.

Dawson, P. J. (2010). Financial development and economic growth: A panel approach. *Applied Economics Letters, 17*(7–9), 741–745.
Eren, B. M., Taspinar, N., & Gokmenoglu, K. K. (2019). The impact of financial development and economic growth on renewable energy consumption: Empirical analysis of India. *Science of the Total Environment, 663*, 189–197.
Fink, G., Haiss, P., & Mantler, H. C. (2005). The finance-growth nexus: Market economies vs. transition countries. *EI Working Paper No. 64*. Europainstitut.
Fuchs-Schündeln, N., & Funke, N. (2003). Stock market liberalization: Financial and macroeconomic implications. *Review of World Economics, 139*(4), 730–761.
Gamra, S. B. (2009). Does financial liberalization matter for emerging East Asian economies' growth? Some new evidence. *International Review of Economics and Finance, 18*(3), 392–403.
Guariglia, A., & Poncet, S. (2008). Could financial distortions be no impediment to economic growth after all? Evidence from China. *Journal of Comparative Economics, 36*(4), 633–657.
Habibullah, M. S., & Eng, Y.-K. (2006). Does financial development cause economic growth? A panel data dynamic analysis for the Asian developing countries. *Journal of the Asia Pacific Economy, 11*(4), 377–393.
Haini, H. (2020). Examining the relationship between finance, institutions and economic growth: Evidence from the ASEAN economies. *Economic Change and Restructuring, 53*, 519–542.
Hasan, I., Wachtel, P., & Zhou, M. (2009). Institutional development, financial deepening and economic growth: Evidence from China. *Journal of Banking & Finance, 33*(1), 157–170.
Hassan, M. K., Sanchez, B., & Yu, J.-S. (2011). Financial development and economic growth: New evidence from panel data. *Quarterly Review of Economics and Finance, 51*(1), 88–104.
Horng, M.-S., Chang, Y.-W., & Wu, T.-Y. (2012). Does insurance demand or financial development promote economic growth? Evidence from Taiwan. *Applied Economics Letters, 19*(1–3), 105–111.
Hossin, M. S. (2023). Interest rate deregulation, financial development and economic growth: Evidence from Bangladesh. *Global Business Review, 24*(4), 690–703.
Hou, H., & Cheng, S.-Y. (2010). The roles of stock market in the finance-growth nexus: Time series cointegration and causality evidence from Taiwan. *Applied Financial Economics, 20*(10–12), 975–981.

Huo, C., Hameed, J., Albasher, G., & Pang, M. (2023). The impact of institutional quality, natural resources, and finance-growth on China's economic recovery: An empirical study. *Resources Policy, 83*, Article 103740.

Jahfer, A., & Inoue, T. (2014). Financial development, foreign direct investment and economic growth in Sri Lanka. *International Journal of Economic Policy in Emerging Economies, 7*(1), 77–93.

Jalil, A., & Feridun, M. (2011). Impact of financial development on economic growth: Empirical evidence from Pakistan. *Journal of the Asia Pacific Economy, 16*(1), 71–80.

Jalil, A., Feridun, M., & Ma, Y. (2010). Finance-growth nexus in China revisited: New evidence from principal components and ARDL bounds tests. *International Review of Economics and Finance, 19*(2), 189–195.

Jehan, Z., & Irshad, I. (2020). Exchange rate misalignment and economic growth in Pakistan: The role of financial development. *Pakistan Development Review, 59*(1), 81–99.

Khan, M. A., Qayyum, A., & Sheikh, S. A. (2005). Financial development and economic growth: The case of Pakistan. *Pakistan Development Review, 44*(4), 819–837.

Lee, C.-C., & Chang, C.-P. (2009). FDI, financial development, and economic growth: International evidence. *Journal of Applied Economics, 12*(2), 249–271.

Lee, C.-C., & Wong, S. Y. (2005). Inflationary threshold effects in the relationship between financial development and economic growth: Evidence from Taiwan and Japan. *Journal of Economic Development, 30*(1), 49–69.

Lee, I., & Shin, J.-H. (2008). Financial liberalization, crises, and economic growth. *Asian Economic Papers, 7*(1), 106–115.

Lenka, S. K. (2015). Does financial development influence economic growth in India? *Theoretical and Applied Economics, 22*(4), 159–170.

Lenka, S. K., & Sharma, R. (2020). Re-examining the effect of financial development on economic growth in India: Does the measurement of financial development matter? *Journal of Asia-Pacific Business, 21*(2), 124–142.

Liu, G., & Zhang, C. (2020). Does financial structure matter for economic growth in China. *China Economic Review, 61*, Article 101194.

Liu, W.-C., & Hsu, C.-M. (2006). The role of financial development in economic growth: The experiences of Taiwan, Korea, and Japan. *Journal of Asian Economics, 17*(4), 667–690.

Ma, Y., & Jalil, A. (2008). Financial development, economic growth and adaptive efficiency: A comparison between China and Pakistan. *China & World Economy, 16*(6), 97–111.

Malarvizhi, C. A. N., Zeynali, Y., Al Mamun, A., & Ahmad, G. B. (2019). Financial development and economic growth in ASEAN-5 countries. *Global Business Review, 20*(1), 57–71.

Mansury, Y., & Sohn, W. (2015). Are financial activities harmful for regional growth? Contradictory evidence from the Indonesian panel data. *Applied Economics, 47*(5), 519–530.

Mohanty, R. K., & Bhanumurthy, N. R. (2019). Analyzing the dynamic relationships between physical infrastructure, financial development and economic growth in India. *Asian Economic Journal, 33*(4), 381–403.

Muhammad, F., Razzaq, N., Muhammad, K., & Karim, R. (2021). Do quality of governance, remittance and financial development affect growth? Evidence from Pakistan. *Estudios de Economia Aplicada, 39* (1), 1–11.

Murari, K. (2017). Financial development–economic growth nexus: Evidence from South Asian middle-income countries. *Global Business Review, 18*(4), 924–935.

Murthy, D. S., Patra, S. K., & Samantaraya, A. (2014). Trade openness, financial development index and economic growth: Evidence from India (1971–2012). *Journal of Financial Economic Policy, 6*(4), 362–375.

Nain, M. Z., & Kamaiah, B. (2014). Financial development and economic growth in India: Some evidence from non-linear causality analysis. *Economic Change & Restructuring, 47*(4), 299–319.

Narayan, P. K., & Narayan, S. (2013). The short-run relationship between the financial system and economic growth: New evidence from regional panels. *International Review of Financial Analysis, 29*, 70–78.

Naveed, S., & Mahmood, Z. (2019). Impact of domestic financial liberalization on economic growth in Pakistan. *Journal of Economic Policy Reform, 22*(1), 16–34.

Nawaz, K., Lahiani, A., & Roubaud, D. (2019). Natural resources as blessings and finance-growth nexus: A bootstrap ARDL approach in an emerging economy. *Resources Policy, 60*, 277–287.

Nazir, M. R., Tan, Y., & Nazir, M. I. (2021). Financial innovation and economic growth: Empirical evidence from China, India and Pakistan. *International Journal of Finance and Economics, 26*(4), 6036–6059.

Nyasha, S., & Odhiambo, N. M. (2016). Financial systems and economic growth: Empirical evidence from Australia. *Contemporary Economics, 10*(2), 163–174.

Ohlan, R. (2017). The relationship between tourism, financial development and economic growth in India. *Future Business Journal, 3*(1), 9–22.

Padoan, P. C., & Mariani, F. (2006). Growth and finance: European integration and the Lisbon strategy. *Journal of Common Market Studies, 44*(1), 77–112.

Peng, J., Groenewold, N., Fan, X., & Li, G. (2014). Financial system reform and economic growth in a transition economy: The case of China, 1978–2004. *Emerging Markets Finance & Trade, 50*(2), 5–22.

Rahman, A., Khan, M. A., & Charfeddine, L. (2020). Financial development–economic growth nexus in Pakistan: New evidence from the Markov switching model. *Cogent Economics & Finance, 8*, Article 1716446.

Ren, M., & Wu, H. (2023). How innovation and entrepreneurship affect economic growth? Government support and financial development as moderators. *Transformations in Business & Economics, 22*(3A), 869–887.

Rousseau, P. L., & Vuthipadadorn, D. (2005). Finance, investment, and growth: Time series evidence from 10 Asian economies. *Journal of Macroeconomics, 27*(1), 87–106.

Sahoo, S. (2014). Financial intermediation and growth: Bank-based versus market-based systems. *Journal of Applied Economic Research, 8*(2), 93–114.

Shahbaz, M., & Rahman, M. M. (2014). Exports, financial development and economic growth in Pakistan. *International Journal of Development Issues, 13*(2), 155–170.

Sharma, R., & Kautish, P. (2020). Linkages between financial development and economic growth in the middle-income countries of South Asia: A panel data investigation. *Vision, 24*(2), 140–150.

Sheera, V. P., & Ashwani. (2014). Financial development and economic growth in India: An ARDL approach. *Finance India, 28*(2), 529–540.

Siddiki, J. U. (2002). Trade and financial liberalisation and endogenous growth in Bangladesh. *International Economic Journal, 16*(3), 23–37.

Siddikee, M. N., & Rahman, M. M. (2021). Foreign direct investment, financial development, and economic growth nexus in Bangladesh. *The American Economist, 66*(2), 265–280.

Soedarmono, W., Hasan, I., & Arsyad, N. (2017). Non-linearity in the finance-growth nexus: Evidence from Indonesia. *International Economics, 150*, 19–35.

Usman, K. (2023). The linkages between trade, financial openness, and economic growth in China: An ARDL-bound test approach. *Journal of Applied Economics, 26*(1), Article 2258616.

Verma, A., & Giri, A. K. (2022). ICT diffusion, financial development, and economic growth: Panel evidence from SAARC countries. *Journal of Public Affairs, 22*(3), Article e2557.

Wadud, M. A. (2009). Financial development and economic growth: A cointegration and error-correction modeling approach for South Asian countries. *Economics Bulletin, 29*(3), 1670–1677.

Wang, N., Shah, M. H., Ali, K., Abbas, S., & Ullah, S. (2019a). Financial structure, misery index, and economic growth: Time series empirics from Pakistan. *Journal of Risk and Financial Management, 12*(2), 1–15.

Wang, C., Zhang, X., Ghadimi, P., Liu, Q., Lim, M. K., & Stanley, H. E. (2019b). The impact of regional financial development on economic growth in Beijing–Tianjin–Hebei region: A spatial econometric analysis. *Physica A, 521*, 635–648.

Williams, K. (2017). Does democracy dampen the effect of finance on economic growth? *Empirical Economics, 52*(2), 635–658.

Yang, Y. Y., & Yi, M. H. (2008). Does financial development cause economic growth? Implication for policy in Korea. *Journal of Policy Modeling, 30*(5), 827–840.

Yao, Y. (2010). Financial intermediation development and economic growth: Does the Chinese counterexample exist? *China & World Economy, 18*(5), 22–36.

Ye, D., Huang, Y., & Ye, X. (2023). Financial structure, technology, and economic growth: A structural matching perspective. *China & the World Economy, 31*(1), 119–148.

Yousaf, A., Bibi, F., & Naz, F. (2021). A cointegration analysis of financial liberalisation and economic growth in Pakistan (1972–2016). *Pakistan Journal of Applied Economics, 31*(1), 77–98.

Zhang, J., Wang, L., & Wang, S. (2012). Financial development and economic growth: Recent evidence from China. *Journal of Comparative Economics, 40*(3), 393–412.

Zhang, L., & Bezemer, D. (2016). Finance and growth in China, 1995–2013: More liquidity or more development? *Cambridge Journal of Regions, Economy and Society, 9*(3), 613–631.

References

Aghion, P., Howitt, P., & Mayer-Foulkes, D. (2005). The effect of financial development on convergence: Theory and evidence. *Quarterly Journal of Economics*, *120*(1), 173–222.

Ahn, C. Y. (2001). A search for robust East Asian development models after the financial crisis: Mutual learning from East Asian experiences. *Journal of Asian Economics*, *12*(3), 419–443.

Aiyar, S. (2001). Growth theory and convergence across Indian states: A panel study. In *India at the crossroads—Sustaining growth and reducing poverty*. International Monetary Fund.

Al-Yousif, K. (2002). Financial development and economic growth: Another look at the evidence from developing countries. *Review of Financial Economics*, *11*(2), 131–150.

Andrews, I., & Kasy, M. (2019). Identification of and correction for publication bias. *American Economic Review*, *109*(8), 2766–2794.

Ang, J. B. (2011). Savings mobilization, financial development and liberalization: The case of Malaysia. *Review of Income and Wealth*, *57*(3), 449–470.

Anwar, A. I., & Mang, C. F. (2022). Do remittances cause Dutch disease? A meta-analytic review. *Applied Economics*, *54*(36), 4131–4153.

Anwar, A., & Iwasaki, I. (2023a). The finance-growth nexus in the Middle East and Africa: A comparative meta-analysis. *International Journal of Finance and Economics*, *28*(4), 4655–4683.

Anwar, A., & Iwasaki, I. (2023b). The finance-growth nexus in Asia: A meta-analytic approach. *Asian Development Review*, *40*(1), 13–48.

A. Anwar, I. Iwasaki, *Meta-Analysis of Finance and Growth in Asia*,
https://doi.org/10.1007/978-3-032-10219-5

Anwar, S., & Cooray, A. (2012). Financial development, political rights, civil liberties and economic growth: Evidence from South Asia. *Economic Modelling*, *29*(3), 974–981.

Anwar, S., & Sun, S. (2011). Financial development, foreign investment and economic growth in Malaysia. *Journal of Asian Economics*, *22*(4), 335–342.

Arestis, P., & Demetriades, P. (1999). Finance and growth: Institutional considerations, financial policies and causality. *Zagreb International Review of Economics and Business*, *2*(1), 37–62.

Arestis, P., Chortareas, G., & Magkonis, G. (2015). The financial development and growth nexus: A meta-analysis. *Journal of Economic Surveys*, *29*(3), 549–565.

Ashton, D., Green, F., Sung, J., & James, D. (2002). The evolution of education and training strategies in Singapore, Taiwan and South Korea: A development model of skill formation. *Journal of Education and Work*, *15*(1), 5–30.

Asteriou, D., Spanos, K., & Trachanas, E. (2024). Financial development, economic growth and the role of fiscal policy during normal and stress times: Evidence for 26 EU countries. *International Journal of Finance and Economics*, *29*(2), 2495–2514.

Bajzik, J., Havranek, T., Irsova, Z., & Schwarz, J. (2020). Estimating the Armington elasticity: The importance of study design and publication bias. *Journal of International Economics*, *127*, Article 103383.

Beck, T., Levine, R., & Loayza, N. (2000). Finance and the sources of growth. *Journal of Financial Economics*, *58*(1), 261–300.

Ben Gamra, S. (2009). Does financial liberalization matter for emerging East Asian economies growth? Some new evidence. *International Review of Economics and Finance*, *18*(3), 392–403.

Bom, P. R. D., & Rachinger, H. (2019). A kinked meta-regression model for publication bias correction. *Research Synthesis Methods*, *10*(4), 497–514.

Borenstein, M., Hedges, L. V., Higgins, P. T., & Rothstein, H. R. (2021). *Introduction to meta-analysis* (2nd edn.). John Wiley & Sons.

Brada, J. C., & Iwasaki, I. (2023). Does financial liberalization spur economic growth? A meta-analysis. *Borsa Istanbul Review*, *24*(1), 1–13.

Cazachevici, A., Havranek, T., & Horvath, R. (2020). Remittances and economic growth: A meta-analysis. *World Development*, *134*, Article 105021.

Chirathivat, S., Rutchatorn, B., & Nakawiroj, W. (Eds.). (2020). *China's rise in Mainland ASEAN: Regional evidence and local responses*. World Scientific.

Chung, P. T., Sun, S., & Vo, D. T. H. (2019). How does financial development interact with economic growth in five ASEAN countries? *Singapore Economic Review*, *64*(3), 441–460.

Cooray, A. (2012). Migrant remittances, financial sector development and the government ownership of banks: Evidence from a group of non-OECD economies. *Journal of International Financial Markets, Institutions and Money*, *22*(4), 936–957.

De Luca, G., & Magnus, J. R. (2011). Bayesian model averaging and weighted-average least squares: Equivariance, stability, and numerical issues. *STATA Journal*, *11*(4), 518–544.

Deidda, L., & Fattouh, B. (2002). Non-linearity between finance and growth. *Economics Letters*, *74*(3), 339–345.

Demetriades, P. O., Rewilak, J. M., & Rousseau, P. L. (2024). Finance, growth, and fragility. *Journal of Financial Services Research*, *66*, 29–49.

Demetriades, P., & Andrianova, S. (2004). Finance and growth: What we know and what we need to know. In C. A. E. Goodhart (Ed.), *Financial development and economic growth: Explaining the links* (pp. 38–65). Palgrave Macmillan.

Doucouliagos, H. (2011). How large is large? Preliminary and relative guidelines for interpreting partial correlations in economics. In *School Working Paper No. SWP 2011/5*. Deakin University.

Errunza, V. (2001). Foreign portfolio equity investments, financial liberalization, and economic development. *Review of International Economics*, *9*(4), 703–726.

Estrada, G. B., Park, D., & Ramayandi, A. (2015). Financial development, financial openness, and economic growth. In *Economics Working Paper No. WPS157543-2*. Asian Development Bank.

George, E. I. (2010). Dilution priors: Compensating for model space redundancy. *IMS Collections*, *6*, 158–165.

Gereffi, G. (2019). Global value chains, development, and emerging economies. In P. Lund-Thomsen, M. W. Hanson, & A. Lindgreen (Eds.), *Business and development studies: Issues and perspectives* (pp. 125–158). Routledge.

Goldsmith, R. W. (1959). Financial structure and development as a subject for international comparative study. In R. W. Goldsmith (Ed.), *The comparative study of economic growth and structure* (pp. 114–123). National Bureau of Economic Research.

Guariglia, A., & Poncet, S. (2008). Could financial distortions be no impediment to economic growth after all? Evidence from China. *Journal of Comparative Economics*, *36*(4), 633–657.

Guo, F., & He, S. (2020). The finance-growth nexus in China: A meta-analysis. *Applied Economics Letters*, *27*(13), 1071–1075.

Gurley, J. G., & Shaw, E. S. (1955). Financial aspects of economic development. *American Economic Review*, *45*(4), 515–538.

Habibullah, M. S. (1999). Financial development and economic growth in Asian countries: Testing the financial-led growth hypothesis. *Savings and Development*, *23*(3), 279–291.

Haini, H. (2020). Examining the relationship between finance, institutions and economic growth: Evidence from the ASEAN economies. *Economic Change and Restructuring*, *53*, 519–542.

Haini, H., Abdul Razak, L., Wei Loon, P., & Husseini, S. (2023). Re-examining the finance—institutions—growth nexus: Does financial integration matter? *Economic Change and Restructuring*, *56*(3), 1895–1924.

Hasan, I., Wachtel, P., & Zhou, M. (2009). Institutional development, financial deepening and economic growth: Evidence from China. *Journal of Banking and Finance*, *33*(1), 157–170.

Häusler, G. (2002). The globalization of finance. *Finance and Development*, *39*(1).

Havranek, T., & Sokolova, A. (2020). Do consumers really follow a rule of thumb? Three thousand estimates from 144 studies say "probably not". *Review of Economic Dynamics*, *35*, 97–122.

Havránek, T., Stanley, T. D., Doucouliagos, H., Bom, P., Geyer-Klingeberg, J., Iwasaki, I., Reed, W. R., Rost, K., & van Aert, R. C. M. (2020). Reporting guidelines for meta-analysis in economics. *Journal of Economic Surveys*, *34*(3), 469–475.

Horie, N., Iwasaki, I., Kupets, O., Ma, X., Mizobata, S., & Satogami, M. (2024). Wage-experience profiles in China and Eastern Europe: A large meta-analysis. *Journal of Economic Surveys*, *38*.

Huang, H.-C., & Lin, S.-C. (2009). Non-linear finance-growth nexus. *Economics of Transition and Institutional Change*, *17*(3), 439–466.

Huo, C., Hameed, J., Albasher, G., & Pang, M. (2023). The impact of institutional quality, natural resources, and finance-growth on China's economic recovery: An empirical study. *Resources Policy*, *83*, Article 103740.

Irsova, Z., Doucouliagos, H., Havranek, T., & Stanley, T. D. (2024). Meta-analysis of social science research: A practitioner's guide. *Journal of Economic Surveys*, *38*(5), 1547–1566.

Isayev, M., & Farooq, O. (2024). The moderating role of shadow banking on the finance-growth nexus. *Applied Economics Letters*. Advance online publication.

Iwasaki, I. (Ed.). (2020a). *The economics of transition: Developing and reforming emerging economies*. Routledge.

Iwasaki, I. (2020b). Meta-analysis of emerging markets and economies: An introductory note for the special issue. *Emerging Markets Finance and Trade*, *56*(1), 1–9.

Iwasaki, I. (2022). The finance-growth nexus in Latin America and the Caribbean: A meta-analytic perspective. *World Development*, *149*, Article 105692.

Iwasaki, I., & Kočenda, E. (2024). Quest for the general effect size of finance on growth: A large meta-analysis of worldwide studies. *Empirical Economics*, *66*(6), 2659–2722.

Iwasaki, I., Ma, X., & Mizobata, S. (2020). Corporate ownership and managerial turnover in China and Eastern Europe: A comparative meta-analysis. *Journal of Economics and Business*, *111*, Article 105928.

Iwasaki, I., Ma, X., & Mizobata, S. (2022). Ownership structure and firm performance in emerging markets: A comparative meta-analysis of East European EU member states, Russia, and China. *Economic Systems*, *46*(2), Article 100945.

Jordan, C., & Majnoni, G. (2002). Financial regulatory harmonization and the globalization of finance. In *Research Policy Working Paper No. 2919*. World Bank.

Kabir, S. H., Al, H., & Hoque, A. B. (2007). Financial liberalization, financial development and economic growth: Evidence from Bangladesh. *Savings and Development*, *31*(4), 431–448.

Kazar, A., & Kazar, G. (2016). Globalization, financial development and economic growth. *International Journal of Economics and Financial Issues*, *6*(2), 578–587.

Law, S. H., Azman-Saini, W. N. W., & Ibrahim, M. H. (2013). Institutional quality thresholds and the finance-growth nexus. *Journal of Banking and Finance*, *37*(12), 5373–5381.

Levine, R. (2003). More on finance and growth: More finance, more growth? *Federal Reserve Bank of St. Louis Review*, *85*, 31–46.

Levine, R., Loayza, N., & Beck, T. (2000). Financial intermediation and growth: Causality and causes. *Journal of Monetary Economics*, *46*(1), 31–77.

Liu, G., & Zhang, C. (2020). Does financial structure matter for economic growth in China? *China Economic Review*, *61*, Article 101194.

Magnus, J. R., Powell, O., & Prüfer, P. (2010). A comparison of two model averaging techniques with an application to growth empirics. *Journal of Econometrics*, *154*(2), 139–153.

Matousek, J., Havranek, T., & Irsova, Z. (2022). Individual discount rates: A meta-analysis of experimental evidence. *Experimental Economics*, *25*(1), 318–358.

McGuire, P., & Conroy, J. D. (2020). Fostering financial innovation for the poor: The policy and regulatory environment. In *Working Paper, Office of Development Studies, Bureau for Development Policy*. United Nations Development Programme.

Mengesha, S. T., & Berde, E. (2023). Financial development and economic growth in Ethiopia: Is there a causal link? *Cogent Economics and Finance*, *11*(2), Article 2245309.

Nazir, M. R., Tan, Y., & Nazir, M. I. (2021). Financial innovation and economic growth: Empirical evidence from China, India and Pakistan. *International Journal of Finance and Economics*, *26*(4), 6036–6059.

Ono, S., & Iwasaki, I. (2022). The finance-growth nexus in Europe: A comparative meta-analysis of emerging markets and advanced economies. *Eastern European Economics, 60*(1), 1–49.

Petrakou, M., Bruno, R. L., & Phelps, N. (2023). The impact of FDI and financial depth on EU regional growth: Income and spatial heterogeneity. *Economic and Business Review, 25*(3), 164–181.

Polák, P. (2019). The euro's trade effect: A meta-analysis. *Journal of Economic Surveys, 33*(1), 101–124.

Porter, T. (2005). *Globalization and finance*. Polity Press.

Rahman, M. M., & Sultana, N. (2024). Nexus of human development and environmental quality in low-income and developing countries: Do renewable energy and good governance matter? *Sustainability, 16*(13), Article 5382.

Rioja, F., & Valev, N. (2004). Does one size fit all? A reexamination of the finance and growth relationship. *Journal of Development Economics, 74*(2), 429–447.

Sahoo, S. (2014). Financial intermediation and growth: Bank-based versus market-based systems. *Margin: Journal of Applied Economic Research, 8* (2), 93–114.

Schumpeter, J. (1912). *Theorie der wirtschaftlichen Entwicklung*. Duncker & Humblot.

Sethi, P., Chakrabarti, D., & Bhattacharjee, S. (2020). Globalization, financial development and economic growth: Perils on the environmental sustainability of an emerging economy. *Journal of Policy Modeling, 42*(3), 520–535.

Sharma, R., & Kautish, P. (2020). Linkages between financial development and economic growth in the middle-income countries of South Asia: A panel data investigation. *Vision, 24*(2), 140–150.

Stanley, T. D. (2008). Meta-regression methods for detecting and estimating empirical effects in the presence of publication selection. *Oxford Bulletin of Economics and Statistics, 70*(1), 103–127.

Stanley, T. D., & Doucouliagos, H. (2012). *Meta-regression analysis in economics and business*. Routledge.

Stanley, T. D., & Doucouliagos, H. (2017). Neither fixed nor random: Weighted least squares meta-regression. *Research Synthesis Methods, 8*(1), 19–42.

Stanley, T. D., & Doucouliagos, H. (2023). Correct standard errors can bias meta-analysis. *Research Synthesis Methods, 14*(3), 515–519.

Stanley, T. D., Doucouliagos, H., & Ioannidis, J. P. A. (2017). Finding the power to reduce publication bias. *Statistics in Medicine, 36*(10), 1580–1598.

Stanley, T. D., Jarrell, S. B., & Doucouliagos, H. (2010). Could it be better to discard 90% of the data? A statistical paradox. *The American Statistician, 64*, 70–77.

Ugur, M., Churchill, S. A., & Luong, H. L. (2020). What do we know about R&D spillovers and productivity? Meta-analysis evidence on heterogeneity and statistical power. *Research Policy, 49*(1), Article 103866.

Valickova, P., Havranek, T., & Horvath, R. (2015). Financial development and economic growth: A meta-analysis. *Journal of Economic Surveys, 29* (3), 506–526.

van Aert, R. C. M., & van Assen, M. A. L. M. (2021). Correcting for publication bias in a meta-analysis with the p-uniform method. In *Working Paper*. Tilburg University and Utrecht University.

Wang, D. K., Cha, H. E., & Seth, N. (2023). How does financial openness affect economic growth at different stages of economies? *Journal of the Asia Pacific Economy*. Advance online publication.

Watson, M. (1999). Rethinking capital mobility, re-regulating financial markets. *New Political Economy*, *4*(1), 55–75.

Ye, D., Huang, Y., & Ye, X. (2023). Financial structure, technology, and economic growth: A structural matching perspective. *China and World Economy*, *31*(1), 119–148.

Zaidi, S. A. H., Wei, Z., Gedikli, A., Zafar, M. W., Hou, F., & Iftikhar, Y. (2019). The impact of globalization, natural resources abundance, and human capital on financial development: Evidence from thirty-one OECD countries. *Resources Policy*, *64*, 101476.

Zaidi, S. A. H., Zafar, M. W., Shahbaz, M., & Hou, F. (2019). Dynamic linkages between globalization, financial development and carbon emissions: Evidence from Asia Pacific Economic Cooperation countries. *Journal of Cleaner Production*, *228*, 533–543.

Zigraiova, D., Havranek, T., Irsova, Z., & Novak, J. (2021). How puzzling is the forward premium puzzle? A meta-analysis. *European Economic Review*, *134*, 103714.

FSC
www.fsc.org
MIX
Papier | Fördert gute Waldnutzung
FSC® C083411

Kolibri 360 GmbH
Ferdinand-Jühlke-Straße 7
99095 Erfurt, Deutschland
produktsicherheit@kolibri360.de